OBJECTIONS TO
NUCLEAR
DEFENCE

Also edited by Nigel Blake and Kay Pole

Dangers of Deterrence: Philosophers on Nuclear Strategy

OBJECTIONS TO
NUCLEAR
DEFENCE

PHILOSOPHERS ON DETERRENCE

Edited by Nigel Blake & Kay Pole

Routledge & Kegan Paul
London, Boston, Melbourne and Henley WITHDRAWN

First published in 1984
by Routledge & Kegan Paul plc

14 Leicester Square, London WC2H 7PH

9 Park Street, Boston, Mass. O2108, USA

464 St Kilda Road, Melbourne,
Victoria 3004, Australia and

Broadway House, Newtown Road,
Henley-on-Thames, Oxon RG9 1EN, England

Set in Times 10/12pt.
by Columns, Reading
and printed in Great Britain
by T.J. Press (Padstow) Ltd, Padstow, Cornwall.

Library of Congress Cataloging in Publication Data

Objections to Nuclear Defence.
Includes bibliographical references and index.
1. Atomic weapons – Moral and ethical aspects –
Addresses, essays, lectures. 2. Deterrence (Strategy) –
Moral and ethical aspects – Addresses, essays, lectures.
I. Blake, Nigel. II. Pole, Kay.
U264.025   1984   172'.42   84-4698

British Library CIP data available

ISBN 0-7102-0249-0 (pbk)

Contents

Acknowledgments   vii

Notes on Contributors   viii

Introduction   *Nigel Blake and Kay Pole*   1

'Better Dead than Red'   *Anthony Kenny*   12

Nuclear Warfare   *Michael Dummett*   28

Nuclear Deterrence and the Use of the Just
   War Doctrine   *Roger Ruston*   41

The Politics of Truth. Exports and Laypeople in the
   Nuclear Debate   *John Krige*   67

Human Survival   *Kate Soper*   86

Morality, Scepticism and the Nuclear Arms Race   99
   Bernard Williams

Morality and Survival in the Nuclear Age   115
   Susan Khin Zaw

The Great Wall of China. Notes on the Ideology
   of Nuclear Deterrence   *Rip Bulkeley*   144

Secrecy, Expertise and Democracy   *Andrew Belsey*   168

Index   182

Acknowledgments

Our great good fortune as editors was to be able to work with such material. The contributors wrote their essays more than a year ago; so, in addition to thanking them for the book we acknowledge their patience with gratitude. When our own patience was flagging and threatening to run out altogether we were each supported by our families – our love and thanks to them. Thanks, too, to the many members of the Open University who commented on the project as a whole, and on some of the content in detail, notably in this respect Greg McLennan and Peter Wright.

We are grateful to Faber & Faber Publishers and Random House Inc for permission to reprint four lines from 'In Memory of W.B. Yeats' by W.H. Auden, from *The English Auden: Poems, Essays and Dramatic Writings 1927-1939*, edited by Edward Mendelson.

Notes on Contributors

Andrew Belsey is Lecturer in Philosophy, University College, Cardiff; his main areas of interest are science and politics and the relations between them. He believes philosophy should combine rigour with concern for important practical issues. He is a member of the Executive Committee of the Society for Applied Philosophy.

Rip Bulkeley has taught philosophy at the University of Khartoum and the Open University. From 1980 to 1982 he worked in Oxford's Campaign ATOM, gave WEA courses in peace studies, and wrote pieces for *Peace News*, *New Radiator*, and *END Bulletin*, as well as unpublished papers on campaign strategy. He has contributed to *CND – The Way Ahead* (eds Phil Bolsover and John Minnion), and is co-author of ' "If at first you don't succeed" – fighting against the bomb in the 1950s and 1960s', *International Socialism*, Winter 1980. Until 1982 he was a member of the editorial collective of *Radical Philosophy*.

Michael Dummett is Wykeham Professor of Logic, University of Oxford. He was fellow of All Souls College, Oxford, 1950-79, and has been a Fellow of the British Academy since 1967. He chaired the unofficial Committee of Enquiry into events in Southall on 23 April 1979 (Report issued 1980). His publications include *Frege: Philosophy of Language* (1973), *Immigration: where the Debate goes Wrong* (1978), *Catholicism and the World Order* (1979), and *Twelve Tarot Games* (1980).

Anthony Kenny is Master of Balliol College, Oxford, where he was Fellow and Tutor in Philosophy from 1963 to 1978. He has written books on Descartes and Wittgenstein and on a number of topics in philosophy of mind, notably *Action, Emotion and Will, Will, Freedom and Power*, and *Free Will and Responsibility*. His article 'Counterforce and Countervalue' on nuclear deterrence, first published in the *Clergy Review* in 1962, has since been reprinted several times.

Susan Khin Zaw is a Lecturer in Philosophy at the Open University. She currently works in moral philosophy, treating the subject in an interdisciplinary manner. She has previously published papers in the philosophy of psychology and biology.

John Krige is the author of *Science, Revolution and Discontinuity* (1980), and has published about a dozen articles in scientific periodicals, as well as several on philosophy of science. He has discussed the dangers of the arms race with several large groups of sixth formers, notably those with an interest in science.

Roger Ruston is a Catholic priest of the Dominican Order who teaches moral theology at Blackfriars, Oxford. He is also a graduate student in the Department of International Relations at Oxford University. For several years he was a member of the Catholic Bishops' Commission for International Justice and Peace and wrote a report for them on the morality of nuclear deterrence entitled *Nuclear Deterrence: Right or Wrong?* (1982). He has written a number of articles on political theology and belongs to Pax Christi.

Kate Soper is a writer, translator and part-time teacher of philosophy at the Polytechnic of North London. She is active in Lewes CND, and was until recently co-secretary of Brighton CND. She is the author of *On Human Needs* (1981) and currently writing a book on humanism. Publications on the issue of nuclear disarmament include an article in *Radical Philosophy*, no. 27 and a contribution to *Over our Dead Bodies* (1983).

Bernard Williams is Provost of King's College, Cambridge. He was chairman of the Home Office Commission on Obscenity and Film Censorship 1977-79. His books include *Morality* (1972),

Descartes: the Project of Pure Enquiry (1978), and *Moral Luck* (1981).

Nigel Blake is Research Fellow in the Institute of Educational Technology at the Open University. He is a philosopher by training and specializes in philosophy of education. **Kay Pole** is Lecturer in the same institute; her background is in psychology and she works with course teams in philosophy, as well as social sciences and education. Both are members of CND. They have jointly edited a companion volume to this one, *Dangers of Deterrence: Philosophers on Nuclear Strategy*, published by Routledge & Kegan Paul in 1983.

Introduction

Nigel Blake and Kay Pole

Throughout the 1980s there has been a growing sense of alarm and unease about the balance of nuclear terror between East and West, fears shared by politicians and soldiers as well as ordinary people. Perceptions of danger and prescriptions for security have varied across the entire conceivable spectrum.

At one end there are those who see the Soviet Union as posing a military threat which endangers not only the West but the entire non-Soviet world (including other Communist states). Those who hold this view typically urge upon us the grim and absolute necessity of military strength for the West, strength of a near-invincible nature. This entails a massive military build-up. It also requires an unprecedented proliferation of new forms of armaments – arms which have military capabilities never known before.

At the other end there are those who believe that the nuclear arms race is inherently unstable, that East-West relations are hopelessly beset by mistrust and paranoia, that our world is an economic and political tinder-box for dangerous conflicts. Without a radical *volte-face* in our political and military stance, we have no hope of avoiding cataclysmic devastation.

Even so, there is not a smooth continuum of opinion between these poles. On the contrary, confusion reigns. Most people seem convinced that the hardline rearmers' views are a recipe for disaster and equally seem sceptical about uncompromising pacifism and nuclear renunciation. But in seeking an honest, well-intentioned and yet practicable position, they face difficulties of several kinds.

One set of difficulties concerns familiar and honest problems –

problems of assessing just which political and military arrangements have a chance of securing a worthwhile peace. If these
difficulties tax the powerful and the well informed, how much
more will they tax the ordinary citizen?

Second, there is a bewildering tangle of doubts about the
proper place of moral considerations in the politics of 'the
Bomb'. Just what is the morality of nuclear deterrence – could it
ever be justified? Are the moral issues themselves issues of
abstract principle or do we need a morality which is firmly rooted
in practical and factual considerations? If the latter, then *which*
practical and factual considerations are most relevant? Is there
really a distinction between a concern for morality and a simple
wish to survive? And if there is, what price morality? Is a
moralizing attitude perhaps a self-defeating one, committing us
all to unworldly policies doomed to promote self-destruction and
ultimate moral disaster?

A third difficulty lies in disentangling the substance of various
views advanced from the undeclared motives of those who
advance them. That there are motives which have little to do with
issues of common survival is frequently, perhaps usually, the
case. And this is not just true of far Right and far Left but of the
general Centre too – centrist politicians have hidden political
agendas and power games to play no less than those they call
extremists.

There is a fourth problem of a rather different kind. When this
book (or rather its close kin) was originally conceived in 1981,
there seemed to be a real doubt as to which way the world would
jump next. The new peace movements were vigorous, expansive
and persuasive; there was room for detailed debate about nuclear
defence issues in many forums and in many countries. Then the
governments of the Right, the staunch proponents of rearmament, seemed precarious, partly because of their rearmament
stance but principally for entirely different reasons. How could it
possibly be that in Britain, for instance, Mrs Thatcher would be
re-elected when unemployment was hovering around the two
million mark? Did this not provide an opening for those who
were urging reconsideration of our defence policies? (And, some
people added, was not the Labour Party the proper and fruitful
arena in which to get things moving?)

We write in the autumn of 1983. Unemployment is now three

and a half million, the opposition parties are in varying degrees of disarray, and we have our answer – Mrs Thatcher could indeed be re-elected. What point is there now in detailed reconsideration of nuclear deterrence when we are confronted with a *fait établi*? Have not the rearmers won? Are not the problems listed above just dead issues?

We present this book in the belief that they cannot be allowed to die. And to keep an issue alive, it is essential to promote its rigorous and detailed examination. If, for the moment, the rearmers have won, plenty of people, by no means all of them nuclear disarmers, will insist that their victory should be reversed.

If the pass has been lost, for instance, on the installation of cruise missiles, that should not prevent anyone asking whether cruise should be allowed to stay or how to remove it. A failure to bargain away SS20s at Geneva will lead to a further twist of the armaments spiral in Europe, and that too should prompt serious debate. (At the time of writing, there are reportedly still plans to increase vastly the numbers of cruise and Pershing IIs in Europe once the first generation has been installed.) The issue of Trident will have to be considered. There are also questions about the strategic defence of the USA and President Reagan's apparent determination to deploy the MX missile, a missile of doubtful use and arguably of danger to its owners. Can this issue be separated from questions about deterrence in the defence of Western Europe? Politicians will attempt to separate them, but we may query the validity of doing so.

We make no apologies, then, for readdressing the issues dealt with in this book. They remain urgent and practically important. Our remaining task in this Introduction is to indicate the relevance of the contributions and the thread of concerns that links them.

This book is a companion to *Dangers of Deterrence*,[1] a collection of essays which appeared in 1983. In the early 1980s, a number of British philosophers established a common belief that the nuclear debate badly needed more contributions from philosophers themselves. They shared an opposition to much, even most, current government thinking, and were most of them in varying degrees committed to the aims of the peace movement. But on the whole they were also unhappy about the conduct of the nuclear debate on both sides. There was a feeling that many of the issues being publicly discussed were at least in part philosophical, but because they were not recognized as such they were extremely badly handled. It was also felt that even where issues were recognized as being properly philosophical, in the discussion of moral questions for instance, the debate was none the less inexpert and would benefit from the participation of professional philosophers. The wide range of apparently disparate issues could not be properly dealt with in isolation from each other, but ought to be addressed between the covers of one book.

Most importantly, the philosophers continue to share a belief that confused thoughts lead to practical mistakes and that practical mistakes about nuclear deterrence may mean the end of us all. Whether the mistakes are mistakes in philosophy or mistakes in engineering or diplomacy is neither here nor there. The philosophers who contribute to this volume and to *Dangers of Deterrence* do so because they believe that it matters to do so. They are not doing philosophy for philosophy's own sake.

Practical considerations prevented the appearance of a single volume containing all the contributions. We hope that readers of this book will also look at *Dangers of Deterrence*, where they will find philosophical treatments of many of the political and strategic questions at issue. That book could be said to address principally the first set of problems which we mentioned above. The present book addresses the second, namely the overarching moral consideration. Here we hope to show that even where interest is focused on the moral questions, the need exists to think carefully about questions of fact – about particular factual issues and about what should and should not be counted as fact. The third set of problems, concerning the credibility of participants in the debate, is implicitly addressed in both books. It should be clear that the essays included in the current book are themselves just as much practical as moral in their concerns. They are not abstract investigations.

In the first paper of the collection, Anthony Kenny begins by analysing various interpretations of the slogan 'Better dead than red'. It is important to do so, he argues, because in at least some interpretations the slogan could be said to be true. However, it is only once this is appreciated that we can clearly see how inadequate it is as a defence of a policy of nuclear deterrence. Though there could well be conditions in which a war against communism were a just war, a *nuclear* war against communism could never be just. To wage such a war would involve the desertion of precisely those values whose defence would otherwise justify going to war in the first place.

It might be answered that while most of us can agree that no such war could be just, this does not refute the claim that nuclear deterrence is necessary in order for war to be averted, that therefore it is justifiable. A fairly orthodox answer to such claims alleges that threats cannot avert nuclear war because they are simply not credible. To launch a first nuclear strike at Russia would only bring destruction down on our heads; whereas a retaliatory strike would by definition be too late to prevent such destruction and perhaps invite yet further punishment.

Kenny notes that the orthodox argument is weak in one respect. Deterrent theorists do not, as the argument supposes, claim that Russia will be disciplined by our *will* to attack or counter-attack. Rather they suppose that it is our mere *power* to use nuclear weapons that will have a deterrent effect. The fallacy in this defence, however, is that power presupposes will. Our mere possession of nuclear weapons does not constitute a power to use them if it is our settled intention never actually to do so. (Kenny notes the impossibility of ever basing nuclear deterrence on sheer bluff.)

The real will to use nuclear weapons which nuclear deterrence requires of us is beyond doubt an evil. Yet apologists for deterrence argue that it is precisely that real will which makes deterrence work; and that the benefits gained by successful deterrence vastly outweigh the gain in moral purity which renunciation of deterrence would bring. Kenny replies that arguments based on the balancing of risks and costs are usually misconceived in practice if not in principle. The risk involved in nuclear renunciation is not that of nuclear attack, but more modestly the risk of nuclear blackmail. And this risk itself cannot be rationally calculated. In the face of such an unknown and possibly slender risk, there is no good reason to abandon a principle central to the Western moral tradition: that it is worse to do wrong than to suffer wrong. To launch nuclear war to resist nuclear blackmail would reduce us to the level of iniquity of our enemy or even worse. Better dead than so.

Michael Dummett asserts the moral wickedness involved in the mere possession of nuclear weapons, let alone their use. He claims that possession reduces us to the same moral level as terrorists. When war was thought to be unavoidable, the ideal was to fight honourably and without hatred – as in ancient times of chivalry. Dummett claims that the Second World War entirely eroded this ideal. The invention and use of nuclear armaments means that war can no longer be conducted solely on the principle of self-defence. Nuclear deterrence puts everyone on a par with terrorists. Laws of War which distinguish between permissible and impermissible acts have no relevance here. Even though the distinctions may be somewhat arbitrary and despite arguments about where the lines are to be drawn, there is no doubt that the use of nuclear weapons is utterly inexcusable. If that can be excused, anything can be excused; morality then has no point. Moreover the possession of nuclear weapons is as evil as their use, for there is an inherent contradiction in the argument that nations can stockpile nuclear arms but never intend to use them. Deterrence based on nuclear arms is necessarily dangerous, he concludes. No conceivable cost or ideological consideration excuses their possession.

The article by Roger Ruston amplifies this. He reminds us that the whole point of the Just War doctrine is to assert the rights of individuals in the face of alleged military necessity. That is the basis of the misunderstood precept of the immunity of non-combatants. He then considers an argument, often used by Western governments to defend themselves from criticism, derived from Just War doctrine. 'Collateral deterrence', they claim, involves a threat proportionate to the expected benefit from deterrence. They concede that the predictable millions of civilian deaths which would be unavoidably involved in a 'tactical' nuclear war would, if they occurred, be disproportionate to any just cause. Yet the whole point of nuclear deterrence is to prevent nuclear war. Thus the threats are undoubtedly propor-tionate to the aim. Ruston denies this. The balance between the nuclear powers is increasingly precarious. Deterrent threats lack credibility; they may therefore fail to deter. If deterrence fails, the use of nuclear weapons entails, as Kenny and Dummett point out, the slaughter of 'innocents' by the million. No just cause could be in proportion to such slaughter.

Practical questions of morality, such as those discussed here, require the assessment of issues of fact no less than of decisions of principle. The broad factual assumptions which inform our first three papers are often challenged by presumptive 'experts'. John Krige's paper discusses the dilemmas facing the morally responsible layman who tries to come to terms with his own lack of 'expertise' and the open disagreement among these supposed experts.

Krige is concerned with the problem of trying to decide whom to believe, and of how experts become accredited as such. He examines the evidence marshalled by successive British governments, which show, it is claimed, that there is a 'Soviet threat' to the Western alliance. He calls attention to the gaps between evidence and conclusions and between conclusions and policy recommendations. The philosophical arguments used to demonstrate the cognitive authority of experts are also called in question. Who are the experts who come to these conclusions, and where does their authority on issues of policy lie?

In a demonstration of the possibility and necessity of confronting the 'experts', Kate Soper takes issue with the celebrated Home Office booklet.[2] She argues that for the government to suggest that its proposals will mean that most citizens of the UK can survive a nuclear attack simply changes the meaning of 'survival'. Life will not be the same. Realistic estimates suggest that our very social structure would disappear, and governments are incapable of imagining ungovernable situations; this perhaps explains their implausible optimism. Nuclear war would destroy the material basis of society and thus the human institutions they support as well. Mere biological survival is what would result, and this would not be distinctively human. Moreover, loss of human values and abilities would make even long-term biological survival most unlikely. In the long run, humans can only survive as humans.

It is accepted by almost everyone that the overriding moral imperative with regard to nuclear weapons is simply to try to avoid nuclear war. Bernard Williams takes issue with our first three contributors, however, for trying to deduce more from this imperative than he believes is strictly possible. His objection is partly that abstract moral principle is no guide to deterrence policy when divorced from consideration of the detailed political and strategic issues. Yet Ruston at least, and perhaps Kenny, would not take issue with that point. (It seems to us that practical considerations are also implicitly acknowledged by Dummett.)

What makes for the real disagreement between Williams and the other three is his scepticism with regard to the variety of politico-strategic analyses on offer and to the complexity of their associated prescriptions. He has to take issue with arguments such as Ruston's not because he dissents from Just War doctrine, but because he believes that nothing can be deduced from it without additional political and strategic premises which are rich in detail yet also well-grounded and broadly beyond controversy.

No such premises exist, Williams claims. So if strategic scepticism is inescapable, and moral certainty unilluminating, what can Britain most reasonably do? In the end it is the very uncertainty of the political and strategic analyses which makes unilateralism the best option for Britain at the moment. The arguments for British unilateralism are less complex than those in favour of retention, rearmament and participation in complex European nuclear strategies and they rest on simpler assumptions; therefore they are less vulnerable to simple human error and miscomprehension. In the present British situation, we have no choice but to take chances. The risks involved in unilateralism are the least dangerous we can currently find.

It could be suggested that Williams demonstrates the moral consequences of the sceptical attitude to expertise advocated by Krige and Soper. Susan Khin Zaw in her turn is sceptical of the view of morality which informs Williams's arguments, no less than the views he attacks.

Khin Zaw divides protagonists in the deterrence debate into crusaders and casuists. Casuists take very seriously the difficulties of establishing detailed and well-grounded strategic analyses. They deplore the emotionality of so much of the peace campaign's words and actions, convinced as they are that emotionality can only obscure issues and mislead people into dangerous strategic errors. If Williams laments the lack of such credible analyses, he shares with the casuists the belief that any such analyses would be centrally important if they were available. Crusaders, by contrast, lack patience with such an approach. They view the entire game of nuclear deterrence as morally rotten at the core and probably fated to end in disaster. On moral grounds we should have nothing to do with it; on practical grounds, we are playing with fire, both figuratively and literally. The moral imperative, according to crusaders, is to walk away from nuclear deterrence as far and as fast as possible. (Dummett's contribution to this volume may be seen in this light.)

In fact, Khin Zaw says, the cooler style of the casuists does not make them superior in rationality. Either side might have the better arguments. (If emotionalism is dangerous, it is not in itself a proof of error.) The emotionalism of the unilateralist crusade is in part provoked by the outcome of rational argument and in part a device in debate whose use can be defended on moral and rational grounds.

Khin Zaw's own sympathies rest with the crusaders. In part at least, their virtue lies in insisting that the moral dimension of our predicament must not and *cannot* be disregarded. It is a constant danger of casuistry that this may happen. But morality is not a Mosaic system of duties and prohibitions. Morality is what most people live by most of the time, and the means by which people make sense of their lives. That is why it creates difficulty for so many – to live by humane values at a day-to-day level, yet collude in the abandonment of those values when matters of military necessity are pleaded.

Khin Zaw emphasizes a further point. Moral values do not exist to make sense of some timeless, unaltering human predicament but to help us make sense of the lives we live here, now. When the conditions of our existence change radically, then our moral values will need to change as well. And arguably our lives under nuclear deterrence are radically different from previously; new values are indeed needed.

Khin Zaw applies these reflections to the nuclear predicament in the following way. Morality cannot be excluded from nuclear strategy because to do so robs the strategy itself of any sense; the abandonment of morality involves the abandonment of the idea of a meaningful future and the abandonment of any point to strategic thinking. And there can be no sense at all to those defences of deterrence which claim to be our best chance whilst agreeing that deterrence may eventually collapse bringing devastation in train. The conclusion, says Khin Zaw, is so absurd that the argument must rest on absurd premisses. If deterrence is as dangerous as that, then it *cannot* be the best chance for the world. To say otherwise is to deny any sense to our lives at all.

A concerted attempt to follow through the programme of revising our sense of values in the manner Khin Zaw advocates would involve a penetrating analysis of the exact nature of our current conditions of existence. Rip Bulkeley argues that the resources of Marxism have more to offer us in any attempt at such an analysis than even Marxists themselves have yet realized.

Bulkeley seeks to understand the economic and social relations which characterize the nuclear state and its typical ideology. He claims that without such understanding, the peace movement cannot hope to promote a world free of nuclear weapons; instead it will get sucked into the debate on how best to use them. Liberal critiques of deterrence (critiques which tend to be casuistical in Khin Zaw's terms) fail to provide appropriate insights. Bulkeley uses the Marxist concepts of inversion and reification to explain the ideology of the nuclear state, and the Marxist concept of class war to explain the posture of nuclear deterrence between the superpowers. Contradiction, in either a Marxist or a logical sense of the term, appears to be an essential characteristic of what we might call 'deterrence ideology'. The ideology is that body of factual assumptions, values and excuses which ruling groups in nuclear states usually invoke to justify their nuclear deterrent postures.

The radical pervasiveness of such contradictions itself requires an explanation. A Marxist explanation of this fact seems to justify revolt, the very price anti-Marxists do not wish to pay. It is hard to avoid the conclusion that the anti-Marxists' best strategy is to find a politico-military doctrine which is not self-contradictory in the ways Bulkeley alleges. That would be the most effective and indeed the most honest way to obviate the need for the kind of analysis he offers.

Non-Marxists will look to find a non-violent manner of working towards the goals of nuclear peace within a framework of democratic institutions. Andrew Belsey argues that this requires the reform of those 'democratic' institutions which we already have, however. Not just any democracy will allow such popular ambitions to be realized.

Belsey sketches two theories of democracy. The liberal orthodox theory, which he calls 'minipart' democracy, allows voting but plays down active participation by citizens in any more detailed decision-making. (Note the extreme reluctance with which any substantive issue of politics is ever put to referendum in Britain.) The alternative, 'maxipart' democracy, involves much greater participation in the democratic process at every level. Yet in British political life, governmental secrecy and the unwarranted authority government accords to 'experts' prevents even minipart democracy from being achieved. Information required to make a rational choice even in voting is not available to the ordinary citizen.

But if human energy is to be directed toward the cause of making peace – a peace, we might add, of the kind ordinary people want – then maxipart democracy is the necessary context for such efforts. And it is just not true, argues Belsey, that the dynamics of deterrence preclude this possible context. The state *can* afford to inform its citizens sufficiently well for them to choose their own destiny without endangering their own security. Nuclear deterrence need not require a closed state. So why not trust the people?

Notes

1 *Dangers of Deterrence: Philosophers on Nuclear Strategy*, London, Routledge & Kegan Paul, 1984.
2 *Protect and Survive*, London, HMSO, 1980.

'Better Dead than Red'

Anthony Kenny

In the course of argument about the morality of nuclear weapons sooner or later the slogan 'Better dead than red' may be introduced. Possibly a defender of the use of these weapons may employ the phrase. Much more likely he may be accused by his opponent of maintaining a position which can be thus summed up. Sophisticated defenders of Western nuclear policy are likely to disown the slogan, but I think it is worth taking seriously because, in my own view, it does contain a certain amount of truth. Like most slogans, it can be taken in many different senses. It is a help in clarifying one's thinking about nuclear war and nuclear deterrence to attempt to sort out in what sense the slogan is true or defensible.

'Better dead than red' may be an expression of preference or the expression of a moral judgment. Most likely it is the latter, but there are many different judgments which it may express. Perhaps it means that one should die rather than become a Communist; or that one should be prepared to kill and die rather than submit to Communist rule; or that it is better that there should be a large number of deaths in a nuclear war than that the West should be overcome by communism. Let us examine various possible meanings of the slogan in turn.

'Better dead than red' may be a dramatic expression of the moral judgment that one ought not to become a Communist. A religious person, believing that to embrace communism is incompatible with his religious beliefs, might affirm that one should be martyred rather than become a Communist. Except on religious grounds it is hard to see how one could substantiate a totally general moral principle that it was wrong to join a

Communist Party: there may well be stages in the history of particular societies in which membership of a Communist Party is preferable to any of the possible political alternatives, and where the injustice of the existing system is so palpable that political inactivity would involve complicity in tyranny. But the record of most Communist Parties which have come to power has been a record of ruthlessness and oppression; and I have no doubt that it would be a disaster for a country such as the UK or the USA to come under Communist rule. Hence I think it quite wrong to join an organization that has such a goal, and I hope I would not do so even to save my life. In that sense, I am willing to subscribe to the motto 'Better dead than red'.

But the slogan, in this sense, is irrelevant to the consideration of nuclear warfare and indeed to almost any real-life situation. Even in the most rigidly organized socialist countries no one is faced with the choice between joining the Party and being put to death. Individuals are indeed forced to make choices between joining the Party and giving up all hope of power and influence; or between joining the Party and losing their friends, their career and perhaps their livelihood. In such circumstances to refuse to join the Party can and does call for heroism, and nobody who has not been faced with the choice can know whether he or she would display the necessary heroism. But 'Better live on bread and water than join the Party' is a moral principle which, however admirable, has clearly nothing to do with questions of the rights and wrongs of nuclear warfare and deterrence.

In fact 'Better dead than red' is more likely to express a principle not about preferring death to becoming a Communist, but about preferring death to coming under Communist rule. It may be a simple expression of preference: 'I would rather die than come under Communist rule.' As an expression of preference, it cannot be used directly to bring pressure to bear on others. It is more important to evaluate it as the expression, not of a preference, but of a moral principle: that one should prefer death to Communist domination.

This principle itself can be taken in several ways. Most plausibly, it means: one should die rather than submit to Communist rule. Someone might hold this in the extreme form of believing that one should kill oneself rather than fall into Communist power. I believe this is a mistaken moral judgment,

13

but I would not wish to argue with people who hold it. They can, when the time comes, act upon their principle without involving us or anyone else in war, nuclear or otherwise, in the meantime.

It is more likely that someone would espouse the principle: one ought to be prepared to be killed rather than submit to Communist rule. This principle, indeed, I myself believe to be correct. That is to say, I think that a citizen of a country such as ours can and should be prepared to risk his life to prevent the country from being invaded by a Communist power or overrun by a Communist insurrection. In saying this, I realize, I am disagreeing with many of those in the nuclear disarmament movement. For many of those who oppose the retention and use of nuclear weapons do so because they are pacifists who oppose all forms of war. I am claiming that pacifists are wrong, and that there can be such a thing as a just war. Moreover, I am claiming that the independence of countries such as the USA and the UK, and the differences between the Communist system and the political system of communism are matters important enough to provide the grounds for a just war.

There can be, I claim, such a thing as a just war: or, more correctly, the making of war can be a just action; it can be morally permissible to go to war. The difference between the formulations is meant to remind us that war is something which is brought about by human beings, is an activity which human beings engage in, and it is that which makes it a topic for moral evaluation. It is wrong to think of war as an impersonal event, something which happens or breaks out like an earthquake or an epidemic. It is not only wrong but dangerous, since it screens one's own and one's country's part in a war from moral scrutiny. A just war is not a war in which both sides are acting justly; on most traditional definitions of a just war that would not be possible, since it is a condition for a war to be just at all that it should be waged in order to right a wrong done, or to prevent an imminent wrong. There cannot be a war which is a just war in the sense that both the combatants are fully justified in fighting war; though, given the complicated nature of international relations, it may well be that both sides reasonably believe they have a just cause. But it can be just to make war in defence against those wo are making war unjustly.

It is dangerous to think of war as an impersonal event: it is no less dangerous to think of it as a self-contained human activity like a game of baseball or cricket. To be justified, war must be an instrument of policy: it must be a means to a desirable, and morally defensible, goal. Victory is not in itself a goal which justifies war; to justify a war one must be able to point to the goods to be achieved by victory. Winning a war is not like winning a game in which the aim is something which is simply defined by the internal structure of the activity. This means that the unconditional surrender of the enemy is not a legitimate objective of war, though one may rightly adopt a policy of unconditional refusal to treat with a particular government. Wars may be waged, not in order to destroy the enemy society, but to force the enemy to desist from the wrong in which he is engaged or about to engage. Spelling out the particular wrong which justifies one's taking up arms is *eo ipso* to spelling out the conditions on which one ought to be ready to accept surrender (plus whatever extra conditions are necessary in order to ensure that the terms of surrender are observed).

Besides the necessity that a war should be waged in order to right a specific wrong, a number of conditions must be observed in its waging if it is to be morally justified. One is that the good to be obtained by the righting of the wrong must outweigh the harm which will be done by the choice of war as a means. Another is that the harm done in warmaking shall be no more than is necessary for the achieving of the legitimate goal of the war. A third, which only partially overlaps with the two previous conditions, is that 'the rule of war' (governing the treatment of combatants and non-combatants, etc.) should be observed.

The provisos which I have specified derive from the reflections of philosophers and theologians on the conditions for a just war, between the Middle Ages and the present century. The thinkers in question were mostly Christians, but there is nothing in their arguments which appeals to specially Christian premises; and several of the rules which they laid down have been embodied from time to time in international agreements. Nations vilify their enemies when they violate the rules of war, and proudly proclaim the fact when they themselves observe them. The rules are not a set of arbitrary prohibitions; they are an articulation of the only conditions under which the international community can rationally accept war, in the absence of an effective supranational coercive force, as a means of righting international wrongs. War is justifiable only if war can be limited, just as within an individual society, police forces are necessary but are tolerable only if there are limits on police powers.

The most important of the traditional conditions for a just war was that it should not involve the deliberate killing of non-combatants. This was sometimes called the prohibition on 'killing the innocent'; but the innocence in question had nothing to do with moral guiltlessness or lack of responsibility: the 'innocent' were those who were not *nocentes*, not engaged in harming your side. Soldiers who had surrendered were, in this sense, no less 'innocent' than infants in arms and had an equal right to be spared. The traditional principle is best formulated thus: it is lawful to kill only those who are engaged in waging war or in supplying those who are waging war with the means of doing so.

The principle, thus formulated, does justify the deliberate killing of more than those who are wearing uniform. It regards as justified, for instance, the killing of munitions workers, or of civilians driving trainloads or truckloads of soldiers. The unintended deaths of uninvolved civilians resulting from an attack on a military target (e.g. the blowing up of a castle, or the bombing of a naval dockyard) were likewise not condemned as murderous by this principle, which was concerned with deliberate killing; though of course they were something very relevant to the question whether the war was doing more harm than good. What was clearly ruled out by this principle was the deliberate massacre of civilian populations or the devastation of whole cities as an end in itself or a means to victory.

It is often said that the conditions for a just war were rules drawn up in a medieval context which are quite inapplicable in modern wars. It is certainly true that the rules are not often observed in contemporary wars; no more were they, for that matter, in the Middle Ages. But it is no objection to a moral principle to point out that people often break it; morals are about what we ought to do, not about what we in fact do. It would be as absurd to say that the rules of war are out of date because people nowadays do not keep them as to say that the law of contract is now superannuated because so many people go in for shoplifting.

But a distinction can no longer be made between combatants

and non-combatants, we are told, because nowadays war is total and the whole community is involved in total war. If what is meant by saying that war is total is that nowadays war is waged *by* whole communities, then it is untrue that any war is total. Even at the point of maximum mobilization in the Second World War a large part of the population of the warring nations consisted of children or of those who were maintaining the services that would have been essential even if the nation had been at peace. If what is meant by saying that war is total is that nowadays war is waged *against* whole communities, this is unfortunately true. The relevant difference between us and medieval society is that we have become technologically so much more proficient at doing this.

But in fact the distinctions on which the rules of the just war were based were clearly applicable in the Second World War. The allies began the war with a cause which was clearly just: to right the wrong done to Poland and to prevent further aggression by an intrinsically evil political system. In the course of the war they violated the prohibition on mass killing on non-combatants not through any inability to notice a distinction between combatants and non-combatants but through a deliberate decision to ignore it. In the case of the UK the decision to change from a policy of bombing military targets to the policy of area bombing of centres of population was an explicit, and bitterly contested, decision at the highest level. In the case of the USA the decision to use the first atom bombs to wipe out the cities of Hiroshima and Nagasaki was taken – on the most charitable version of events – on the basis of a cool calculation that the devastation of these centres of population was the speediest way of ensuring a victorious end to the war.

Even in the nuclear age the distinction between a policy of attack on military targets and one of attacking centres of population is a very clear one. In the days when Mr McNamara was secretary of defense we were taught to distinguish between a counter-force nuclear strategy, aimed at knocking out the enemy's strategic forces, and a countervalue strategy, aimed at destroying his cities. More recent US secretaries of defence have distinguished between 'soft targets' (the urban-industrial base of society) and 'hard targets' (missile silos and command/control facilities). So that even in the nuclear age the conditions for a just

17

war are relevant; they are not antiquated in the way, say, that a rule that one should not take arms against one's feudal overlord would no longer have any application.

I have spent time sketching the just war tradition because I believe that it still provides the best theoretical framework within which to consider questions of right and wrong in warfare, and because it is important to show that the choice is not between espousing pacifism on the one hand and endorsing the nuclear strategy of the Western alliance on the other. Having argued that some wars *can* be just, I shall not spend time in defending the position which I have also maintained, that a (conventional) war to defend the UK and the USA from Communist domination *would* be just, provided that the rules of war were observed. There are, perhaps, few who would both accept the doctrine of the just war and deny that such a war fell within the bounds of a just war; but in any case the serious question is not whether a conventional war, but a nuclear war, would be justified in defence of the West against communism.

It is in this sense that the slogan 'Better dead than red' encapsulates a certain type of defence of Western nuclear policy. The differences between the Communist system and our own are such, it is maintained, that to prevent the evil of having communism imposed upon us we would be justified not only in going to war, but in waging a war which would violate the traditional rules for the conduct of wars: a war of mass destruction and indiscriminate killing. Better for everyone – both on our side and on theirs – to be dead than for us to be made red, than for us to have Communist rule forced on us.

I have been at pains to elucidate the senses of 'Better dead than red' in which it contains some truth because in this most important sense it enshrines a monstrous falsehood. No doubt a nuclear war could be waged in which only military targets were attacked: a war which ended after a first-strike exchange upon hardened silos in Montana and the Urals. If it was for this purpose that nuclear missiles were being stockpiled on both sides, the arms race would be comparatively harmless and totally pointless; and the dictum 'Better dead than red' would be irrelevant to it. But the nuclear strategy which the stockpiles serve is one which involves as an option, at one or other stage, the use of weapons to destroy large centres of population, and to bring an enemy society to an end.

The exercise of this option is something which nothing could justify. The differences between the West and the Warsaw Pact nations are of two kinds, material and non-material. Western nations enjoy a number of material advantages by comparison with their Eastern counterparts: they can be summed up by saying that we have in general a far higher standard of living. More important, in the West we enjoy a large number of freedoms of which those living in the Soviet bloc are denied, and this facilitates the pursuit of many values which we cherish.

Nuclear attack on an enemy population is not justified by the defence of either of these advantages. Perhaps few would seriously maintain that one can justly inflict a horrible death on millions poorer than oneself in order to protect the differential between one's standards of living. But the defence of Western non-material values is equally impotent to provide a justification for nuclear massacre. Respect for innocent human life and for international law is no less a part than freedom of speech or rights against arbitrary arrest of what gives us a right to cherish and defend the values of Western democracy. To the extent to which we forfeit our respect for life and law we forfeit our claim to have any moral superiority to defend against Communist threat. As for democratic institutions, few of those are likely to survive a war in which both sides suffer nuclear devastation; to keep life going at all after such a catastrophe is likely to demand a social organization more ruthlessly authoritarian than anything now to be found on either side of the East-West divide. Even if the West by some miracle escaped devastation, so that the slaughter was one-sided, it would end the war having by its own act destroyed the claim that it possessed a system of human values which was worth defending; its institutions would deserve no more respect or loyalty than those of Hitler's Germany.

It would perhaps be very widely agreed – in the UK if not everywhere in the USA – that the waging of nuclear war would be wicked folly. Even a Conservative government pamphlet setting out to defend the British independent deterrent begins by saying 'Talk of fighting a nuclear war is dangerous nonsense, because there can be no winners in such a conflict.' It is no wonder, however, that there is a spate of books describing the horrors of nuclear war; for it is necessary to keep reminding people of what the world would be like after a nuclear war in order to bring home to them that there is no desirable goal which can be rationally pursued by launching such a war.

But while admitting that the actual waging of a nuclear war would be pointless as well as immoral, there are many who defend the manufacture and stockpiling of nuclear weapons as a deterrent. Thus the pamphlet already quoted says: 'the strategy of deterrence has held firm, despite the increasing international tensions of recent years, because it would be madness for either side to launch an attack on the other.'

If this is how the strategy of deterrence is enunciated, there seems a paradox at its core. If A tries to deter B from something by threatening to launch a nuclear attack on B, A is threatening to do something which on A's own account it would be madness for him to do. If B thinks that A means what he says, B must think that A is mad; if B thinks A does not mean what he says, then B must think that A is bluffing. Either way, then, B must think that A is either mad or lying: so how is A's threat supposed to provide a reason for B to act or to desist from action?

Perhaps when the Conservative government says that it would be madness for either side to launch an attack on the other, what it really means is that it would be madness to launch a first-strike attack on the other side, thus inviting nuclear retaliation. A second-strike attack, in retaliation upon a first-strike attack from the other side, is perhaps not, in the government's view, something to be regarded as madness; and it is *this* which provides the deterrent to a first-strike Soviet attack.

But would it, in fact, be a rational action for a country which had undergone a first-strike nuclear attack to launch a retaliatory nuclear attack? This seems to be quite widely assumed. Thus Senators Kennedy and Hatfield, in a book urging its readers to halt the arms race and support a nuclear freeze between the USA and the USSR, say: 'an all-out Soviet nuclear attack against the US would precipitate massive retaliation by American nuclear forces against the Soviet Union.'[1] The book questions many of the assumptions of current US and British defence policy, yet the authors enunciate this as if it was not in any way one of the assumptions which needs rethinking or questioning.

But would it, in fact, be the rational thing to launch a retaliatory strike if one had suffered the unimaginable horrors of a full-scale nuclear attack? A retaliatory strike could, of course, be viewed as an act of revenge; but few politicians, during peacetime planning at least, are willing to present revenge in and for itself as a respectable goal of policy. Otherwise than as an act of revenge, a retaliatory strike would seem to be at best pointless, and indeed against the striker's own interest considered from even the most strictly selfish point of view. A second strike would have no deterrent effect. It would by this time be too late for deterrence to have any force; it would not be like the punishing of criminals within a local society, too late indeed to prevent the crime which is being punished but calculated to teach a lesson to the individual criminal for the next time, and to all other citizens for the future. It would act against the interest of the striking nation; it would decrease the possibility of the survivors of the strike which has already been suffered receiving the medical assistance and economic aid which they will need if they are to rebuild anything of their stricken society.

The differences which at present exist between, say, the USA and the USSR would be insignificant in comparison with the differences between the USA as it now is and the USA as it would be after absorbing a full-scale nuclear attack, or the differences between the USSR as it now is and the USSR as it would be after such an attack. From the point of view of material civilization and technology, once the USA had suffered a nuclear attack, the nearest thing there would be to the original USA would be the as yet undestroyed industrial society of the USSR; it would be this hostile but kindred society which would provide the best hope, in the long run, of any eventual reconstruction of the USA along the lines of the rehabilitation of Germany and Japan by the allied powers after the Second World War. From the non-material point of view, of course, the USA after having absorbed a nuclear attack from the USSR would have an enormous moral advantage over its enemy in that it was not – yet – guilty of mass murder on a scale unparalleled in history. But *that* advantage is precisely what it would throw away, in a matter of minutes, by launching a retaliatory attack. And it would be thrown away without the slightest prospective material advantage in return.

If both a first-strike and a second-strike use of nuclear weapons would be irrational, how can it be rational to possess them at all? How can it fail to be mad and wicked to threaten what it would be mad and wicked to do?

Thus runs a popular argument in favour of unilateral nuclear disarmament. The argument is powerful, but it is as it stands too simplified. It fails to take account of the fact that a power which has the capacity to retaliate with nuclear weapons is less likely to be attacked by another nuclear power than one which has no such capacity. The unilateralist needs to have a convincing answer to the question, frequently put by Lord Chalfont and others, 'Would the USA have used atomic weapons against Japan in 1945 if the Japanese had had the ability to retaliate in kind?'

The reason that the possession of nuclear weapons by A works as a deterrent on B is that B *does not know* whether or not A will be mad enough, when the time comes, to launch a nuclear counter-attack. It is a nation's power, rather than its willingness, to use nuclear weapons, which is the essence of the deterrent. And however wicked it may be actually to use nuclear weapons against cities, however wrong it may be to be willing to do so, how can the mere possession of a power be something which is immoral in itself?

To answer this question, several points have to be borne in mind. First of all, if our enemies do not know whether we would retaliate by bombing their cities, neither do we. This is so whether 'we' means the electorate, the military command, the cabinet or the prime minister. Even the president of the USA does not know what any of his successors would actually do in the event of a Soviet attack on the USA; he does not know what orders he would himself give in any actual crisis. There exist, of course, many strategic plans worked out in detail; but which of them, if any, is ever put into execution no human being can foretell.

It is sometimes argued by moralists that a deterrent policy is a policy of bluff, and this must be wrong since bluff involves lying. This seems wrong. The deterrent policy would be one of bluff if our leaders knew that they would never give orders for a second strike. I wish it were a policy of bluff, but it is not: our leaders do not know what they would do, but they certainly do not rule out even in the privacy of their own minds the possibility of actually carrying out the threats which their policy involves. Lying is wrong, but the wrongness of lying is very much less than the

22

wrongness of the intention to commit mass murder. That is why I wish that the deterrent policy were one of bluff.

But in any case, a deterrent policy need not involve any lying at all. Twenty years ago, in an excellent essay on Morals and Nuclear War the Revd Herbert McCabe OP wrote as follows:

> In order for [nuclear weapons] to be a deterrent you would have at least to pretend by lying that you would use them and lying – like the little girl in Rikkiti Tikkiti Tin – we know is a sin. This argument will not do because we do not in fact need to tell lies about our intentions. If I have rockets with nuclear warheads pointing at Moscow, however much I claim that my Christian morality would debar me from using them, Kruschev is going to be deterred from launching his. The Deterrent Theory therefore survives this criticism.[2]

The real reason why the maintenance of the power to destroy an enemy population is immoral is that in order for the nation to have the power, individuals in the nation must have the willingness to exercise the power. Everyone involved in the military chain of command from the top downwards must be prepared to give or execute the order to massacre millions of non-combatants if ever the government decides that that is what is to be done. It is true that this is a conditional willingness: it is a willingness to massacre if ordered to do so. It is true that it is accompanied, in every member of the armed forces I have ever spoken to, by a profound hope that those orders will never be given. None the less, it is a willingness which is required and insisted upon in all the relevant military personnel.

This is what is really wrong with the deterrent strategy. To a pacifist, who thinks there should not be armies, navies, or air forces at all, it probably seems no great extra iniquity that the military should be trained in readiness to massacre. To someone like myself, who thinks that the military profession is in itself an honorable and indeed noble one, it is very horrible that we should be following a policy which makes it a mark of the good serviceman to be willing, in the appropriate circumstances, to commit murder on a gigantic scale.

As I have said, a policy of bluff would be preferable to a policy of deterrence which involves a serious intention to carry out a second-strike threat. But a policy of pure bluff is not really possible. The secret that there was no real intention to honour the second-strike threat could never be kept. It would have to be kept to very few indeed if the power to carry out the threat was to be maintained. It would have to be kept, not only from the enemy, but from the deterrer's own population and agents. It would, in particular, have to be guarded from every member of its armed forces. In any case, an administration which, *per impossibile*, kept secret its own firm intention never in any circumstances to use nuclear weapons would have to pass this information on eventually to the succeeding administration if the bluff was to be maintained; and it could not bind these successors to secrecy to ensure that the policy remained one of bluff rather than of solid intent.

Defenders of the deterrent will argue that the conditional willingness to engage in massacre which is an essential element of the policy is a slight and almost metaphysical evil to weigh in the balance against the good of preserving peace. The moral blemish which this may taint us with in the eyes of the fastidious is at best something to be put on the debit side, along with the financial cost of the weapons system, against the massive credit of maintaining our independence and our security from nuclear attack. Unilateral disarmament might perhaps make our hands a little cleaner and save us some disagreeable expense; but so far from reducing the risk of war it might actually bring it nearer.

A defender of the deterrent may well admit that all-out nuclear war is a greater evil than Communist domination: not all deterrent theorists believe that it is better to be dead than red in that sense. But though nuclear war is worse than Communist domination, it is argued, unilateral disarmament presents a much greater risk of Communist domination than the maintenance of deterrence does of nuclear war. Suppose, for the sake of argument, that nuclear war is ten times as bad as Communist domination; still, unilateral disarmament makes Communist domination virtually certain, while maintenance of the deterrent presents no more than a 1 per cent risk of war. Hence the deterrent policy is ten times as rational as unilateral disarmament.

Many arguments of this pattern have been presented: the mathematics naturally varies from this simple form, and the particular odds and valuations can be the topic of lengthy argument. But the most commonly heard arguments against unilateral disarmament take the form of an appeal to two kinds of risk: the risk of nuclear war, or the risk of Communist hegemony.

Talk of the risk of war involves the fallacy of considering war as a self-generating event like a storm. It takes more than one side to make a war; a nuclear war would have to be something we were a party to no less than our enemies. The risk of nuclear warfare is not something which can be assessed without reference to our own future policies and decisions. This may seem to be a quibble: maybe our enemies cannot go to war with us without our complicity, but they could certainly attack us without our leave, and from a selfish point of view it is the risk of nuclear attack which is to be feared, every bit as much as the risk of a two-sided nuclear war.

However, even the craziest enemy is unlikely to launch a nuclear attack for no reason. He is likely to do so either in retaliation, or to gain some military or political objective. We can avoid attack of the first kind by avoiding first-strike action of our own; we can avoid an attack of the second kind by conceding the political or military objective to the enemy before he attacks. (If he is so crazy that he will attack us for no reason whatever, then no policy we can adopt is likely to deter him either.)

The risk that we incur if we disarm is not a risk of nuclear war nor of nuclear attack; we abolish the first by disarming and we can avoid the second by surrender. If we disarm, what we bring closer is not war or nuclear catastrophe: it is the possibility of nuclear blackmail, of being forced to surrender by the mere threat of nuclear attack.

Nuclear blackmail is not at all an impossible policy for an enemy to adopt; it is not even necessarily an irrational one for a nuclear power to adopt against a non-nuclear power. It will be remembered that it was advocated by Bertrand Russell: before the USSR produced its first atom bomb Russell counselled that the West should take advantage of its atomic superiority by threatening to bomb the USSR if it would not agree to international arms control. His suggestion was not taken, even though the Western powers had just emerged from a war in which they had shown no lack of willingness to employ strategic

Anthony Kenny

bombing as a policy for victory. It is indeed striking that the two superpowers, since they have had nuclear weapons, have never explicitly resorted to nuclear blackmail against non-nuclear powers, even when they have been fighting, and even losing, conventional wars with them.

It is not easy to assess the degree of danger of nuclear blackmail to a country which lacks nuclear weapons. In so far as we encourage other nations to sign non-proliferation treaties, we regard it as a danger which countries other than ourselves should be prepared to face. The USA and the USSR each believe that the other aims at world domination. I doubt whether the USA does and I do not know that the USSR does; no doubt it would like every other nation to be ruled by a pro-Soviet government in the same way as the USA would like every other nation to be ruled by an anti-Communist government. It does not follow that the Soviet Union would be prepared to use nuclear blackmail to make every country into its puppet in the way that the Warsaw Pact countries are its puppets. But that is certainly a possibility which cannot be ruled out. Nobody really knows how much of present Soviet aggressiveness is due to a desire not to be in a position of disadvantage in comparison with a hostile nuclear superpower. It is romantic to believe that it would altogether disappear if the USA ceased to be a nuclear threat; but it is surely equally unrealistic to think that it would persist totally unaltered.

In the end there is no denying that total unilateral disarmament by the Western powers would leave them vulnerable to Soviet nuclear blackmail if the USSR retains its nuclear arsenal. This risk, I believe, is one which should be faced: it is a terrible risk but a risk less terrible than that of nuclear war. For our nations to be reduced to the status of Romania would be far less of a disaster than for all our cities to be reduced to the condition of Hiroshima and Nagasaki in 1945. The degree of risk of the two courses is not something that can be quantified in any scientific way. Whatever the Pentagon computers may simulate, what will eventually happen will depend on unpredictable human decisions on both sides. But one thing is clear: accepting the risk of nuclear blackmail does not involve giving a blank cheque to *our own* leaders to commit mass murder in the event of war.

26

Attempts to base nuclear strategy on the calculation of risk leave out of account the most important thing. This is the principle, basic to European morality for centuries since its enunciation in ancient Athens, that it is better to be wronged than to do wrong. That principle holds good even when the wrongs in question are, considered in isolation from the question of who perpetrates them, comparable in scale. But of course the wrong we would do, if we used nuclear weapons in a major war, would be incomparably greater than the wrong we would suffer if the worst came to the worst after nuclear disarmament.

I have considered various senses of the dictum 'Better dead than red' and have tried to draw various morals from what is true in that dictum. Of course, the slogan may be used not to express a moral judgment at all, but merely to give utterance to a personal preference. If someone tells me that he would prefer to be killed in a nuclear attack than to be subject to Soviet hegemony, who am I to disbelieve him? But such a preference, if it is seriously thought through, can hardly be very widely shared. The inhabitants of Warsaw already suffer what we would have to suffer if we surrendered to Soviet nuclear blackmail. Yet in the worst days of martial law, can anyone really believe that what the Polish dissidents would really have liked would be for the West to put them out of their agony by dropping a nuclear device with the centre of Warsaw as Ground Zero?

Notes

1 E.Kennedy and M.O. Hatfield, *Freeze! How can you help prevent Nuclear War?* Bantam Books, 1982.
2 Revd H. McCabe OP, 'Morals and Nuclear War', *Blackfriars*, XLII, November 1961.

Nuclear Warfare

Michael Dummett

War has for so long – throughout history, and surely throughout much of prehistory – been a part of human existence that we have forgotten to be surprised by the fact. Every so often, a large body of human beings abandon their normal conduct towards some other large body of human beings, and, instead, employ every means, or almost every means, within their power to kill and mutilate the others in large numbers, to destroy their cities and their economy. During such periods of war, normal human reactions to the enemy population are turned upside down. People who, in peacetime, would manifest the proper feelings of horror at some air disaster cheer when they see on their cinema screens some poor wretches plunge to earth in a burning plane. Young men, taught as children to show consideration and sympathy for others, are berated by army sergeants when, at bayonet practice, they fail to display adequate feelings of bestial hatred towards the imaginary Germans or Russians, represented by stuffed dummies, into whose bellies they are plunging their blades. Of all the many appalling facts about the conduct of human beings to one another, this is surely the most appalling; but we have long ceased to be appalled. It is, without doubt, to our credit as a nation that, during the last war, we recognized the existence of those unable to accomplish the reversal of normal behaviour expected of the majority, and registered them as conscientious objectors; it remains the prevalent appraisal that pacifists are cranks, people who have failed to shake off the naiveté of childhood. Believers in world government are generally understood to be cranks, too. Such people want to put an end to war. They have noticed that, wicked or stupid as those in charge of, say, a county council may be, and great as is the harm they can inflict on those over whose lives they have a say, they neither start building camps within which to exterminate some section of their population nor invade a neighbouring county with armed forces, at the same time dropping bombs on the county town. They have concluded that it is not because members of county councils are, in general, less wicked than members of national governments that they do not do these things, but simply because they lack the opportunity, and would be stopped at the very start of preparations for doing them; and they conclude that national governments must be placed in the same position. Simple-minded, no doubt, many of these advocates of world government are, but they have at least addressed a question to which most people think it not worth while attempting to give an answer, namely how can wars be prevented? It testifies to our acceptance of war as a permanent, inescapable feature of human life that we see no point in asking such a question and give not a moment's thought to finding an answer to it.

Even if it were not rendered obvious by the existence of nuclear weapons, it would need no acuteness to see that the continued occurrence of wars is something we cannot afford to tolerate, not merely because it is intrinsically intolerable, but because of the steady increase in the frightfulness of war due to advancing technology. It is a commonplace that a war fought with the nuclear weapons that now exist would, at the very least, be an unparalleled catastrophe for the human race; in face of this, most people simply avert their minds from the possibility. What rational attitude is it possible to take?

In wartime, we often take, and are encouraged to take, an attitude to the human beings who are our enemies more callous than that of a whaler to the whale, in that we derive positive enjoyment from their sufferings. We do not do so consistently, however: we so respond to anything presented to us as a victory or success, but, left to ourselves, we have some human feelings towards them still. At the back of our minds, perhaps right at the back of them, but still present, there is, or has been until recently, the dream of chivalry. We know we have to fight: but, knowing that, we should like to be able to fight without any hatred in our hearts, without degrading ourselves by picturing

29

our enemies as devils or as vermin, but continuing to recognize them as human beings and continuing to have towards them the attitude that any human being ought to have to another. We should like to respect our enemies, though thinking them misguided and believing it necessary to stop them doing whatever it is that we oppose. That is the chivalrous ideal: if both take that attitude to each other, they can engage in honourable combat; either may, in the course of it, kill the other, since that is what the conflict in their aims has come to, but, if both survive, then, the combat over, they can behave to one another with courtesy and even compassion. That is how it is in the romances. Though the combat is mortal, it is hedged about with rules that make it fair combat: two men – two knights – may fight all day to the death, but neither will attack the other from behind or when he has dropped his sword, and, if one is unhorsed, the other will dismount. The precise rules do not matter; what matters is that there are rules, and it is by observing these rules that the combatants raise themselves above the level of a pair of wolves tearing at each other, and make it possible to see them as fighting without malice towards one another, but as honourable servants of conflicting causes.

In what other frame of mind could anyone who professed to be a Christian possibly undertake so horrible a business? He has committed himself to loving his enemies, therefore he can involve himself in severing their heads from their shoulders or burying his bayonet in their guts only if he can love them while doing so. How can he do that unless by treating the dream of chivalry as reality? Indeed, what other attitude is possible for anyone, Christian or not, who considers himself to be what we are accustomed to call 'civilized', though indeed the modes of behaviour so described are not more characteristic of societies that have attained the level of complexity known as civilization than of those we describe as 'primitive'? No doubt it is humanly impossible for anyone whose life is at stake and who has seen his comrades lose theirs to fight and still hold those he is fighting in high regard; no doubt the ideal of chivalry was never more than dream. Certainly such events as the massacre of the inhabitants of Jerusalem when the Christian knights entered it as the climax of the First Crusade made a bitter mockery of the whole conception, of chivalry and of crusade alike. But still, we have had that dream, if only at the back of our minds; our having it is as important to our history as our acceptance of war as inevitable and as something one may decently bring about or take part in, if only because it was the condition for the latter attitude.

The dream of chivalry became, in the hands of the moral theologians, the doctrine of the just war; but I have preferred to speak of the former because it has influenced many, whereas the theological doctrine has had little effect save on theologians. It is common to both that there are rules of war: the just war requires, not only a just end, but also just means, which entails that, no matter how righteous your cause or how desperate the danger in which you stand, there are things you cannot do even if it means losing the war. Let us pick out just two of these. You may not mistreat or kill prisoners of war, or those seeking to surrender; and you may not mistreat or kill non-combatants. When we entered the Second World War, these two principles were still generally accepted among us. It was a standard comment by the press on the German bombing raids to cite it as characteristic of Nazi barbarity to attack civilians. That was the war that ended with Hiroshima and Nagasaki: but of course our government and air force had long abandoned any scruples of this kind. The public had not, however. There was a quite deliberate attempt by our government and press to conceal from the British public what the British air force in particular, and the allies in general, had been doing to the cities of Germany and, later, of Japan. The attempt was not wholly successful; but it did in considerable part screen us from the knowledge of the scale and ruthlessness of the attacks upon civilians that we were making.

There was, therefore, for the public at large, no decisive moment of change; no point at which the political or military authorities declared their repudiation of the belief that the deliberate massacre of civilians, of women, children, old people and any others not engaged in combat, was not a legitimate means of waging war. Rather, we slid into a new attitude, eased into it by slogans about 'total war' and 'there are no civilians nowadays'. No one stood against it; no one said that we were committing crimes of just the kind that, not long before, we had instanced as proving Nazi barbarism.[1] And, at the end, we were faced with the commission, by our allies the Americans, but with

31

the full connivance of our government, of two such crimes on a scale hitherto unimaginable. We could not, after six years of war, allow ourselves to think that we had proved ourselves to be criminals as much as those we had been fighting. We had fought the war in the conviction of moral superiority. We had been liberating Europe from Nazi barbarity (our role in Asia was, indeed, more dubious); we had inaugurated war crimes trials to prove it: the thought that we had sunk as low as those we were putting on trial had to be rejected, and hence the destruction of the two Japanese cities accepted as legitimate acts of war. The brainwashing was complete. Perhaps if just one person with moral authority – the Pope, for example – had declared unequivocally that these were monstrous crimes, the brainwashing would not have been quite so complete. We should, no doubt, have rejected the charge with indignation, but we should have retained uneasy consciences. But the Pope was silent, and so were all who might have spoken, and who should have spoken. And so the change of mind became irrevocable. Henceforth, there would be no more civilians; henceforth, all means of war were legitimate.

Our world has inherited the consequence of this; not yet, thanks be to God, the massive consequence of another use of nuclear weapons, but many smaller consequences. As everyone says, one of today's great problems is terrorism. But what is terrorism? It is not like murder, or theft, or rape. Someone who has committed a murder knows that he has done so – at least if it is a straightforward murder of someone neither an infant nor incurably ill. But terrorism is, of its nature, a crime that only other people can commit, in the sense that only other people can be elsewhere. An objective definition of terrorism, as it used to be understood, might be as a means of conducting civil or guerrilla warfare, or organized insurrection, by deliberately killing and injuring innocent people. Such a definition fastens on the means, not on the cause. It makes sense only on the assumption that there are means that are not to be employed, however just the cause. But we do not believe that: we destroyed any such belief together with the cities of Hiroshima and Nagasaki. So we cannot define terrorism in that way: we can distinguish 'terrorist', 'guerrilla', 'freedom fighter' only by reference to our own sympathies and antipathies. So, whatever I do, *I* cannot be a terrorist, any more than I can be an extremist: I can only be what other people, with their distorted perception, believe to be a terrorist or an extremist. Mrs Thatcher's indignation at murders by the IRA is not, indeed, a phoney indignation, but an unprincipled indignation, like a soldier reacting to the death of a comrade by saying, 'I'll get those bastards'; she has no grounds on which to disapprove of similar actions by those whose cause she favours. No one committed to defence by nuclear weapons can have any principled objection to murder.

The principle of the old restrictions upon whom one may lawfully kill in war was that it is legitimate to kill somebody only when he is attacking you (and then only if that is the only effective way of stopping him). As a principle governing individual conduct under personal attack, this draws a reasonably clear line between murder and killing in self-defence, but in war it has never been taken literally: no army officer would attempt to apply it from occasion to occasion. To do so would rule out a surprise attack, or indeed a counter-attack after a lull. If it were said that the mere presence of soldiers on the soil of a foreign country could be construed as their being continuously engaged in attacking that country, it would still follow that no forces could pursue their attackers across the frontier. The conventional answer to this has been that a nation engaged in a just war must offer its opponents reasonable terms, and may continue to fight, on the opponents' territory, until these are accepted; an enemy's refusal to make terms is thus interpreted as a kind of attack, even by those in fact in headlong flight. The obligation to offer reasonable terms was a further casualty of the Second World War, with the allies' demand for unconditional surrender; the Korean war provided a perfect example of the crossing of a frontier for purposes of conquest or retribution.

It is not humanly possible for individual soldiers, or officers commanding platoons, companies, battalions or armies, to abide by or refer to the principle of self-defence. For this reason, the conventional rules of war substituted for it rules that could be applied more mechanically: so long as a state of war existed, one might kill members of the enemy forces in uniform unless they were surrendering or had surrendered. Perhaps moral theologians unswayed by the need to justify the actions of the State might have had trouble with such an adaptation of their principles: perhaps deeming men to be attacking you when they are in fact resting or running away was not strictly defensible. But, if it was to be possible to fight wars at all, the principle required some modification; better to modify it into a code that might in practice be observed than to draw no line between war and licensed wholesale murder. The code was far from being scrupulously observed, particularly by the strong against the weak, above all by imperial powers against those they made their colonial subjects. Until the Second World War, however, it was theoretically acknowledged.

'There are no civilians nowadays.' The suasions that were used for abandoning the code were all of this 'Where do you draw the line?' variety, a variety exceedingly familiar in ethical discussions. In ethics, the law of excluded middle must hold; at least, it must hold for an agent engaged in deciding what to do, if not for someone judging actions already taken by others. In a concrete situation, a given course of action must be evaluated either as morally permissible or as morally impermissible; it is not possible to treat it neither as to be considered nor as not to be considered. Casuistry, considered as a branch of ethics, is concerned entirely with drawing the line in the various regions which that line must traverse. For almost every ethical principle, the line determining its application will lie in swampy ground.

As an argument for drawing no line at all, for abandoning a moral principle altogether, the question, 'Where do you draw the line?', is almost always to be rejected, however difficult it may be to answer as a question in casuistry. That is not to say that, understood as playing the former role, it is always footling: when it is used in ethics, we cannot always simply dismiss it, as we often can in non-ethical applications, by saying that, hard as it may be to draw the line, there are things obviously on one side of it and things obviously on the other. There are surfaces which are unquestionably red and others which are unquestionably orange; but we can rest content with acknowledging that no sharp line can be drawn, that there are surfaces neither definitely red nor definitely orange, though definitely either one or the other. It is just because we can rest content with this that the question,

'Where do you draw the line?', has no force whatever against the assertion that the pillar-box is red. When the issue is a moral one, however, we cannot allow that the line is blurred, that an action may with equal justice be said to be wrong or not to be wrong: and so a doubt whether a line can be drawn calls in question the principle which requires it to be drawn.

The force of the question should nevertheless not be exaggerated. The best way to counter it is, of course, to answer it, to show that there is a way of drawing the line that is not merely arbitrary. When we do not know how to do this, it is a matter of conflicting intuitions: the intuition that the moral principle is correct, and that there must therefore be a way of drawing the line that determines its application in difficult cases, even if we do not know exactly how to do that, versus the intuition that there can be no reasonable way of drawing the line, and that therefore the principle must be false. The opponent of the principle has to do more than show that the defender of it does not know how to draw the line: he has to show that no line could be drawn, and this is quite as hard as drawing it. It is possible also for the defender to hold that we have here come upon the limits of moral generalization. It is in specific instances that the law of excluded middle applies; it is far less clear that there must be some formulation detailed enough to decide every instance in advance.

Thus, although the question, 'where do you draw the line?', has more bite in moral contexts than in most, inability to answer it should never lead us to reject clear moral intuitions; above all, not the intuition that it is the horrible things that people do to one another in war that require justification, rather than not doing them. Where nuclear warfare is concerned, we do not need to know where to draw the line. We do not need to know whether the code formerly acknowledged by all, even if frequently violated, went too far in reinterpreting the principle of self-defence; we do not need to answer those who say that it did not go far enough. We do not need to question whether the bombing of a munitions factory is a legitimate act of war; or whether, if so, the killing of the munitions workers is to be justified by the principle of double effect, or whether such workers can be regarded as a sort of combatant out of uniform. Whatever the answers to these questions, it is crystal clear that the obliteration of whole cities, and the indiscriminate killing of civilians, regardless of age, sex or occupation, constitutes mass murder: that for no end whatever could anyone excusably take part, or acquiesce, or risk taking part or acquiescing, in such an act.

No subtle arguments are needed to reach this conclusion. We do not need to delineate the limits of a just war, and so deduce the conclusion from the doctrine so formulated: if this is not beyond the limits, there are no limits. To recognize that nuclear warfare is unconditionally wrong, we need to know only two things: that the same moral principles that govern all our lives apply to governments and to acts committed at the command of governments; and that therefore war does not suspend those principles. If the obliteration of whole cities, or whole populations, is not murder, there is no such thing as murder; if it is not wrong, then nothing is wrong. That is, there is nothing that one may not lawfully do in order to gain sufficient advantage for oneself, or at least to avert sufficient ill from oneself. 'We are fighting a war, too bad for those who get in the way,' captured terrorists say when asked if they feel remorse for their bombings; agents of security forces who have practised torture would doubtless reply in the same vein. To these no one who would in any circumstances condone the use of nuclear weapons can say any more than, 'I happen to be on the other side.'

The commission of acts of monstrous wickedness drives the perpetrators in some degree insane. (Probably this is also true, in the corresponding degree, of acts of petty wickedness.) Immediately after the end of the war with Japan, President Truman made a speech in which he blasphemously praised the wisdom of the Almighty in putting such terrible weapons in the hands of a people, the American people, too humane to use them. The USA is the only nation that has so far actually used nuclear weapons, and we in Britain belong to a nation that shared the complicity in their use. The world is as it is precisely because the only time a nation has had an opportunity to use such weapons against an enemy that could not retaliate, it did so; if it had refrained, all our expectations would now be different.

The justification now offered for possessing nuclear weapons is, of course, as a deterrent. I have not come across anyone who condemns the dropping of atomic bombs on Hiroshima and

Nagasaki as a crime, but nevertheless defends the possession of nuclear weapons as a deterrent; an argument based solely on deterrence is to that degree likely to be hypocritical. However, it is the deterrence argument which is responsible for the acquiescence of the bulk of our population in the spending of vast sums by our government on these horrible weapons. Does the consideration that they are not intended for use, but to prevent others using them, affect the moral conclusion?

As I have heard a bishop argue in this connection,[2] it is far from obvious that it is always wrong to threaten what it would be wrong to do. The argument applies, however, only to individuals, not to governments. An individual may know that his threat is idle; a government cannot make idle threats, because the actual orders will soon be known to the other side's intelligence services, and because no government will remain indefinitely in office. Deterrence can work, if at all, only if there is an actual intention to retaliate. This means that it is useless to possess nuclear weapons unless there is a conditional intention to use them, at least if the other side uses them first. But to use them in any circumstances would plainly be a crime, and an enormously horrible one. It would be, and was, wicked to use them in order to win a war; it would be equally wicked to use them because, by having had the intention to use them in retaliation, one might have prevented their use against oneself, although, by hypothesis, one has failed to do so.

For these reasons, no government could combine possession of nuclear weapons with an intention in no circumstances to use them; yet more obviously, no government which had such an intention could declare it. It is therefore preposterous to defend possession of these weapons as a threat that would not be carried out: no ordinary person could have any ground for assuming that it would not be carried out. All this applies even if one's government is to be trusted, and no government is to be trusted. Politicians, in power or out of it, lie as a matter of course, a fact to which there are countless attestations. No one could trust their assurances that nuclear weapons were to be used only in retaliation. We already know, from what happened at the end of the Second World War, that British and American politicians would have no scruples about using them if they thought they could get away with doing so. Since we know this, and since in any case the use of such instruments of mass murder is morally forbidden even in retaliation, we all have an absolute moral obligation to take any action in our power to prevent Britain from possessing nuclear weapons, or allying herself with, or providing bases for, any country that possesses them. Until our country is no longer potentially involved in conducting nuclear warfare, we also all have an absolute obligation not to join the armed forces; whether you yourself take part in the use of morally prohibited means of warfare or not, you are implicated in the use of them if you fight in a war in which there is a foreseeable likelihood of their being used. It is true that a soldier does not abrogate his responsibility for obeying criminal orders but, by becoming a soldier, he knowingly puts himself in a position in which he will find it extremely difficult to disobey, and in which he may be given orders whose significance is not explained to him.

But would not the effect of unilaterally disarming and of disengaging from NATO and the alliance with the USA be to present our country on a plate to the Soviet Union? It seems extraordinary unlikely unless the rest of Western Europe followed our example – but what if it did? It still seems unlikely to me that the Soviet Union would want to add to its troubles by extending its domination to the rest of Europe, even if it could discount the danger of American intervention; and that is all we have to fear from giving up nuclear arms, since we have already found ourselves powerless to prevent Soviet actions in Hungary and Czechoslovakia. I should think the greater danger would be American attempts to destabilize or wreck the economies of neutralist Western powers, but I really do not pretend to know what would happen. We are not here in an area where the reckoning of consequences is appropriate. The obliteration of whole cities, let alone of an entire population, is not an open option, to be taken if the consequences of not doing so would be bad enough for us. It is obviously and unconditionally wicked, and therefore not to be contemplated as a possible course of action.

In any case, why are we so special? A Soviet occupation would, without doubt, be grim, and would involve a severe curtailment of the liberties of all and the unjust imprisonment and gross ill treatment of some. But it would certainly be no worse than the régime of the colonels in Greece, engineered by the CIA and sustained by American foreign policy, for the defence of which an exercise was staged by NATO. It would be vastly better than the agony inflicted on the people of Chile in the aftermath of Allende's overthrow, for which Kissinger claimed credit during the 1972 election campaign, or than that now being inflicted, with our government's approval, on those of Guatemala and El Salvador, or than the régime of Pol Pot, whose overthrow the Western governments refused to recognize, or, for black people, than the cynical oppression to which, in South Africa, they are subjected by a system kept in being by the USA and Western Europe. Occasionally some squeamishness is manifested about the supposed 'double standard'; but there is no double standard, only ruthless and single-minded power politics. All ideological content was long ago squeezed out of the cold conflict with Russia: we are against the Vietnamese because they are allies of Russia, and in favour of the Chinese, and of anyone they favour, because they are hostile to Russia. We are not engaged in the defence of liberty: we are concerned to defend only *our* liberties, and to do so at whatever cost in suffering to the weaker peoples of the world. It is not to be questioned that the Soviet régime is an oppressive one, and has imposed and maintained oppressive régimes in other countries. But no unbiased judgment could deny that the USA, either by government policies or by the operations of the CIA, which no president dares to check, has been a yet greater menace to the freedom of other nations, installing and maintaining, by direct intervention, 'destabilization' and economic manipulation, the most diabolical régimes based on torture and murder. By allying ourselves with such a power, and condoning its policies, even with an occasional ineffective squeak of protest, we have placed ourselves in a position in which, in any future war, even our cause would be tainted and unjust.

The only possible moral policy, for the present, is to act to prevent our country from continuing to have anything to do with nuclear weapons. To work, as far as possible, against the political and economic oppression of a large part of the world's population is not a separable duty; for the West generally, and our country in particular, is in large measure responsible for all that misery. The policies which cause it spring from the very same source as our involvement with nuclear weapons, namely an insane determination to see that we are all right, while letting the rest of the world go hang. That is only for the short term. So negative a course of action provides no adequate long-term strategy. Those who dare not abandon the policy of deterrence can do no more than hope that it will stave off a nuclear holocaust for – well, for how long? For another few decades? Do they dare to hope, for as long as a century? Say a century (which is *very* optimistic) – what is supposed to happen then? What future does mankind have? A century is nothing in the life-span of the species – can we hope for no more? Extinction, or reduction to barbarity, or, at best, a crime so hideous that no one will be close to sanity for generations; one of these things in, at most, the lifetime of our children's children's children, and perhaps far sooner – is that the only future they have to offer to the human race? We *have* to find a way of making war of any kind impossible. I do not know how it is to be done, but it *has* to be done. Those who devise nuclear strategies and talk of megadeaths are already insane. That great majority who accept the idea of deterrence and avert their minds from thinking further about nuclear warfare are simply too terrified to face reality. How, then, are we to find a way out of this appalling impasse unless some people think about, and then start working for, a means to bring war to an end? No one can do this but those who have the sanity and courage to disengage themselves from the whole monstrous business; and their disengagement will be pointless unless they also do precisely that.

Editors' Notes

1 As a matter of record, Bishop Bell, with the support of Archbishop Lang, regularly questioned in the House of Lords the necessity and morality of Bomber Command's area bombing activities from 1942-4. Bell's was an informed criticism; he was in personal contact with Liddell-Hart who was nurturing doubts on the issue.
2 The editors received Professor Dummett's paper six months before the Bishop of London also endorsed this argument.

Nuclear Deterrence and the Use of the Just War Doctrine

Roger Ruston

At their best, arguments put forward in support of nuclear deterrence have considerable persuasive force and I do not believe they proceed with complete disregard for moral principles. But I do believe they misapply them through lack of realism at several different levels. The arguments are severely affected by failure to comprehend the likely outcome of any use of nuclear weapons in war and a failure to appreciate the historical tendencies of the degenerative condition which we call 'nuclear deterrence'. The net result is an inability to make correct judgments about the ethics of nuclear deterrence according to the widely accepted principles of international morality contained in the doctrine of the Just War and partially embodied in legal form in the International Laws of War. I refer to principles relating to *jus in bello* rather than those relating to *jus ad bellum*, i.e. the just conduct required of any party fighting a war, whether or not their cause is a just one. The likelihood of any war being fought with regard for justice depends not only upon what is done in the heat of battle but also – and increasingly in modern times – upon the preparations which precede it. The fundamental moral decisions are made when we develop, manufacture and deploy the weapons, rather than when they are used in the anger and confusion of war. It will then be too late for any significant moral decisions.

The main lines of the argument for possession of a nuclear deterrence force by the Western alliance may be summarized from official and other authoritative British sources as follows:[1]

1 The nuclear deterrent system, in which the world is divided

into nuclear-armed blocs, each with the capacity to destroy the other in an all-out war, is by no means the ideal way of maintaining world peace. It is however the best way in the present circumstances since

2 we cannot now go back on the awful invention of nuclear weapons. The achievement of weapons of ultimate destruction in 1945 permanently changed the nature of war. The world now has to live for ever with the possibility of their use.

3 The prevention of any war between major powers has now become the central purpose of the deterrent system. Even so-called conventional war must not be allowed to happen since its destructive power has vastly increased since the Second World War. Moreover, a conventional war in which one side was facing non-nuclear defeat would be the surest pathway to nuclear war.

4 Therefore, the best way to make sure that nuclear weapons are never used is to maintain the nuclear balance, in which both sides know that any use of the weapons would be met with such appalling consequences that they would never dare to embark on aggression. If aggression did occur through some dreadful miscalculation of our resolve, we have a series of nuclear responses available from the 'tactical' to the 'strategic' which would make any aggressor think again before provoking an all-out war which nobody could win. (This is the strategy of 'flexible response'.)

5 If prevention of war is our main goal, there is an alternative to nuclear deterrence: non-resistance to aggression. This would have to be complete non-resistance in the military sense, since any armed conflict would risk the use of nuclear weapons against a country which did not possess them. However, the Western alliance is facing a threat from an alien and ruthless system of government in Soviet communism, which has shown itself to have no regard for human freedom and lives if they get in the way of state policy. Since the Soviet Union and its allies have a large nuclear armoury, the West, if it got rid of its nuclear weapons unilaterally, would leave itself effectively defenceless. The Soviet Union could then work its will on us, either through invasion or, more likely, through nuclear blackmail.

6 Even if the present Soviet leadership is not planning

aggression against us, there can be no guarantee that in the future a more belligerent leadership would not do so. Recent history has taught us that we live always with the possibility of facing a ruthless dictator such as Stalin or Hitler, who may kill millions of people in pursuit of his political ambitions.

7 Our – that is, NATO's – nuclear deterrent therefore guards us against both destructive war and domination by murderous régimes. To renounce it would leave us effectively defenceless and open to both these fates. It remains therefore, *the lesser of the evils* with which we are faced; that is, to continue making threats of nuclear retaliation in case of attack is a lesser evil than inviting destruction or domination through unilaterally abandoning our deterrent weapons. It is therefore the moral option we must continue to take.

8 The absence of war between the great powers for 36 years is eloquent testimony to the effectiveness of nuclear deterrence in preventing war. Moreover, careful management of the system will ensure that it continues to work in the future since the penalty for allowing it to break down would be mutual annihilation.

The argument for the British *independent* nuclear deterrent involves further steps which I shall not consider here. I will not attempt to examine the above argument point by point, but instead will examine some of the assumptions upon which its ethical status depends. I choose three in particular: (1) the system of nuclear deterrence is not based on bluff; (2) the system is stable and will remain so; (3) the evil of using the weapons in war could be a lesser evil than not using them. The first two assumptions are of a technical nature, but they bear directly on our final judgment of the morality of nuclear deterrence itself. The third is a moral assumption in itself which can only be accepted or rejected on the basis of certain moral principles governing warfare. I shall appeal to a proper use of the Just War Doctrine in order to do this.

The system of nuclear deterrence is not based on bluff

This is obviously true and it is only wishful thinking on the part of some Christians that makes the point worth discussing. No system could be based on bluff which depends upon the willingness of hundreds of people in the chain of command to obey orders which would result in the weapons being fired. They are chosen and trained for their willingness to do this. Bluff could never be a national policy. This means that a moral case for retaining nuclear weapons cannot rest upon driving a wedge between use of the weapons in combat and possession of the same weapons for deterrence only, as if these involved two quite separate moral intentions. The conditional intention to use the weapons is inseparable from possession. If we agree to possession, the conditional intention of those who command and operate them in our name is our intention too. We may not therefore disengage our consciences from a future use of the weapons by claiming that we agree to deterrence but not to use of the weapons in war. Therefore, if we accept deterrence, we must accept that there could be a situation in which use of the weapons would be morally justified (the third assumption). Deterrence is designed to prevent it, but deterrence might break down. On the level of actual policy, it is well known that the NATO alliance reserves the option of first use of its nuclear weapons in the event of Soviet aggression in Europe. The credibility of the NATO defence system depends upon a real willingness to exercise this option.

The system is stable and will remain so

This assumption is highly questionable. No one claims that the system is completely fail-safe, but its supporters do claim that it is stable enough: that we can safely say that the risk of the weapons being used with it is much less than the risk of a major war occurring – probably involving nuclear weapons – if we were to renounce them unilaterally.

The supporters of the prevailing policy of nuclear deterrence also tend to assume that it is 'delicate' rather than 'robust', which seems at first sight to contradict the claim that it is stable. But perhaps delicacy and stability are rightly distinguished, even if neither of them – or only one – is actually true of nuclear deterrence. 'Stable' seems to mean: will last into the foreseeable future as a means of avoiding war, on condition that the East-West balance is scrupulously maintained by the appropriate arms modernizations, etc. On the other hand, 'delicate' seems to mean: prone to dangerous situations if this condition is not fulfilled and the balance is not maintained. That the system should be claimed to be delicate as well as stable is important for two purposes: (1) as a justification for the competitive aspects of the nuclear arms race, and (2) as a strong argument against unilateral reduction by the West.

My argument will not be about the delicacy of the system but about its supposed stability. I leave the question of delicacy open.[2] It seems to me, however, that an obsessive attention to the supposed delicacy is: (1) a block to any effective disarmament since it props up the myth of multilateral disarmament, and (2) a factor which contributes to decreasing stability as each side tries to outpace the other in technical advances in the name of maintaining the balance. The introduction of MIRVd missiles is the classic example of such a destabilizing change.

It is clearly important for the ethical status of nuclear deterrence that it should be stable. If it carried within it the seeds of its own breakdown, it would tend to undermine the argument from the lesser of two evils. We would find it increasingly difficult to claim that we were staving off a greater evil by keeping it, unless we believe that mutual annihilation – even when it is brought about by the system itself – would always be a better fate than Soviet domination. A belief of that kind would put us outside rational argument altogether.

Stability has both short-term and long-term aspects. By short-term stability I mean the risk of accidental use of the weapons – the risk of it being triggered by such things as computer errors, insanity, natural disasters and the like. I will not discuss this in detail. There is much disagreement about it and nothing can ever be proved until such time as something disastrous happens. There is some evidence that both the USA and the Soviet Union may be developing 'launch-on-warning' plans for fear that their land-based missiles might be destroyed with the highly accurate MIRVd missiles now deployed on either side. And the Soviet Union has shown some public alarm at the deployment of Pershing II missiles close to their borders on account of the very short flight time to their centres of power – about 4 to 5 minutes.[3]

45

This could provoke a launch-on-warning policy. Such technical developments as this make mistaken reactions to misunderstood signals all the more likely.

However, it is the evidence against long-term stability that is the more alarming. By long-term stability I refer to the claim that nuclear deterrence can be continued indefinitely into the future without any structural decay of the system leading to nuclear war. There have recently been many grave doubts passed on this by military men and independent analysts on both sides of the Atlantic, who probably know what they are talking about. Few of them are in favour of unilateral disarmament, but they are all convinced that the vast growth and diversification of nuclear arsenals has decreased, not increased, world security. They ought to be taken seriously.[4]

There are at least three good reasons for thinking that nuclear deterrence is not a stable state which can be indefinitely maintained, but that it is on the contrary a degenerative state which is increasingly difficult to maintain. These are:

1 The arms race, which continuously undermines security through the competitive development of new weapons systems. The question is, can the nuclear powers maintain the nuclear arms race – which has already produced many times the number of weapons needed for deterrent purposes – without one side or the other being driven into a situation in which it might appear to be the right time to use its weapons in a pre-emptive strike if it does not want to see them destroyed at their bases? It is highly unlikely that either side would do such an irrational thing in time of peace, i.e. wage preventive war; but in time of great international tension nations do irrational things. The development of multiple, independently targetable warheads has made pre-emptive strikes a real possibility. A nation at war might decide to take the consequences of retaliation if it thought it could eliminate the bulk of its enemy's nuclear force before part of that force was used against its own weapon bases. It may only be a matter of time before technical advances take away the invulnerability of missile-submarines. President Carter's 'Presidential Directive 59' which restated the policy that US nuclear forces were to be aimed 'primarily at military targets' certainly provoked the

Soviet leadership into thinking that the USA was providing itself with a first-strike capability.

2 Proliferation of nuclear weapons to other countries, particularly those such as Israel, Libya, Iraq, India, Pakistan and South Africa, who live in a state of continual enmity with their neighbours. There is little doubt that some of these countries would use nuclear weapons if they were losing a conventional war and that international involvement in these areas would make it most unlikely that the conflict could be contained. The Non-proliferation Treaty has not been a great success in its main objective, as two review conferences have shown. Critics from non-nuclear countries see a direct relationship between the failure of the nuclear powers to curb their nuclear arms growth and the relentless spread of nuclear technology and materials and doctrines of deterrence to other parts of the world.

3 The development of weapons apparently designed for fighting wars rather than for deterring them. This includes tactical and battlefield weapons now integrated at many levels of NATO and Warsaw Pact forces in Europe. The chief danger is that it erodes the borderline – or 'firebreak' – between conventional weapons, which may be used to fight wars, and nuclear weapons, which may not. It exposes one of the main contradictions at the heart of nuclear deterrence: the search for credibility leads ·to the production of 'usable' weapons, which produces the dangerous illusion that nuclear war can be fought and won.[5] This undermines the deterrent role of nuclear weapons: the more credible the weapons are as a deterrent, the more they have to look as if you would use them; the more usable you try to make them, the more you believe you can use them, the more they are likely to be used in the end. Moreover, they cause a radical confusion between defence and offence. They are said to be purely defensive, yet they cannot be used for any rational defence – at least, on land. They can only appear as offensive weapons to the other side and are therefore highly provocative. Whatever the real intention, it is obviously important for the effectiveness of deterrence – which is always a message conveyed to a potential enemy – that the right message is getting across. War fighting weapons convey a confused and provocative message. It has

been one of the constant internal confusions of nuclear
weapons policies from the start that two contradictory aims
have been pursued: on the one hand, really effective
deterrence, and on the other hand (usually by the military),
usable weapons with which battles can be won.[6] Unusable
weapons go deeply against the grain of military mentality. At a
time of great international tension and war-fever there would
be pressure to use some of the thousands of tactical nuclear
weapons which have long been part of war plans – especially
by the side which found itself losing a conventional engage-
ment. This is perhaps the most likely pathway to nuclear war
in Europe.

While on the subject of stability, it is worth pointing out a
curious feature of the official case for deterrence: the main
argument in support of stability is an *a priori* one which shows
little regard for the way human beings behave. The argument is
that no one would dare to use the weapons since the
consequences to themselves would be so appalling. Therefore the
system is safe. I have never thought this to be a good argument.
It is rather like arguing that no one would dare to commit murder
if capital punishment were reintroduced. It is arguing what is the
case from what ought to be the case if everyone were perfectly
rational. It takes no account of the fear, irrationality and
despairing desire to 'get it over with' which grip people and their
leaders in time of international crisis, especially at the culmin-
ation of a propaganda war and an arms race. It is an argument
for chess-players only.[7]

If we believe that the use of our nuclear weapons now targeted
on the Soviet Union would never be morally acceptable and that
any moral weight that possession of the weapons has depends
entirely on their capacity to prevent war, then even a small
degree of instability would cause grave moral doubts about it, to
say the least. But a final judgment about this will depend on what
we decide about the third assumption which I mentioned above.

The evil of using the weapons in war could be a lesser evil than not using them

If deterrence is not a bluff and if it is not entirely stable, then we must face the moral implications of using the weapons if the worst comes to the worst. We have the conditional intention of using them and the conditions may materialize. There are two declared goals of NATO nuclear policy: preventing war and preventing Soviet aggression. NATO has long since made the option to rely on a nuclear defence of Europe. Under some unforeseen circumstances the two goals may conflict and the choice will have to be made. Therefore, if we come to the conclusion that use of the weapons could never be morally acceptable, we must likewise conclude that possessing the weapons for deterrent purposes is not morally acceptable. In which case the argument would collapse which claims that nuclear deterrence is the right course to take because it is the lesser of two evils.

There are at least two important conditions for making that argument work. The first is a condition for all arguments which aim to identify the right course of action as the one which involves the lesser of two evils: namely, that when we make comparisons between evils – as we must often do in morals – we are comparing non-moral (or 'pre-moral') evils, not moral ones. We are trying to find out what the morally right course is, not what the least morally wrong course is.[8] Utilitarians will reject these conditions as meaningless, since they will say that everything is in the balance until a decision is made about relative consequences and that the right course is that which has the least bad consequences, measured in numbers of deaths or something of the kind. I shall maintain – along with the Just War tradition – that there are some things which may never rightly be done, or even contemplated, not because consequences do not matter, but because some actions are unacceptable consequences in themselves, whatever the initial justice of one's cause. Acts of war which indiscriminately kill non-combatant civilians are of this kind. This includes using any kind of weapons indiscriminately, so as deliberately not to distinguish between military and civilian targets, but also using weapons which are virtually certain to be indiscriminate in their effects because they cannot be used in any other way.[9]

The second condition relates to the morality of threats, or conditional intentions to cause harm: namely, we must make an accurate reckoning of the most probable course of events, should the conditions materialize and the threat be carried out. Above all, in matters of warfare, we must avoid making a judgment which is based on hypothetical possibilities which are unlikely to be realized in practice. We must get out of the imaginary realm of logical possibilities where the debate about nuclear weapons so often takes place. We must not base our judgment on what might be done, for instance, with single nuclear shots against ships at sea, or 'surgical strikes' against isolated military bases, or 'warning shots' which suddenly make our enemies completely rational – and similar fantasies. It is not what might *conceivably* be done with nuclear weapons which is the important thing to consider – it is what is *most likely* to be done with them in the event of war. We must think only in terms of nuclear forces as they actually exist, as they are now deployed and targeted and as they are most likely to be used in the course of a serious conflict between East and West. In any case, it is not the moral aspects of this or that type of nuclear weapons which are important, but those of an entire nuclear arsenal and strategy which – according to the doctrine of flexible response – is all of a piece.

If it is virtually certain that putting the deterrent threat into practice would involve us in actions of great wickedness, then the threat itself must be judged to be a wicked one, whatever we say is the real motive for making the threat. There are of course some actions harmful to others which may be justified as punishment for offences committed, and they may legitimately be threatened beforehand as a deterrent. This is particularly true of 'defence deterrence', namely the threat that an attack upon us would be resisted at such great cost to the attacking forces that it would not be worth their while to make the attack. But there are other actions which cannot be justified as punishment on failure of deterrence, either because they are in themselves morally repugnant or because they are out of all proportion to the offence committed. Therefore it cannot be right to threaten them. This is especially true of threats to harm third parties – hostages. Thus it would be wrong to try to coerce the government and armed forces of a state into refraining from evil against us by threatening to destroy their civilian population, either directly or through actions against their centres of power which would inevitably have the same effect. I am referring to the principles of discrimination and proportionality which occupy a central place in the modern Just War Doctrine in both its Christian and secular forms. There are some current arguments which seek to avoid these conclusions which I shall consider below. Meanwhile it is important to decide to what extent nuclear deterrence is actually 'hostage deterrence' rather than simply 'defence deterrence'.

It is clear that nuclear deterrence does not *necessarily* rest upon threats to blot out cities full of non-combatant civilians as such. It does however rest upon threats to blot out cities because they are centres of state power. This is either because the cities themselves hold vital centres of government or military power – as do London and Moscow, for instance; or it is because centres of military power and communications are very near to cities, as the fallout blows. It is sufficient to remind ourselves that the entire recent debate about the merits of the Chevaline warhead modernization for Britain's Polaris missiles centred upon the question of whether or not it had the chance of penetrating the defences of Moscow, that centre of Soviet state power, containing millions of people. Dr David Owen said that it was not worth the cost and that other – less well-defended – Soviet cities should be targeted instead.[10] To claim that strategic nuclear weapons would be used in a way that discriminates between military and civilian targets is a theoretical claim only. As Lord Zuckerman reminds us in his recent book:

In view of the enormous size of the nuclear armouries . . . one dare not lose sight of the fact that from the operational point of view there is practically no difference, apart from the verbal one, between what is now called counterforce and what is termed countervalue. . . . There is built into nuclear weapons greater destructive power than is necessary for military purposes, and their secondary, non-military effects overshadow those which relate specifically to their military use.[11]

A recent US Congress study of the effects of nuclear war examined counter-force attacks against missile silos, bomber bases and submarine bases in the USA and the Soviet Union. The most important feature of such attacks is that they would have to comprise a large number of ground bursts in order to be effective in destroying military targets, especially hardened missile silos. This would produce 'intense fallout, causing most of the damage to the civilian population, economy and society'. Counter-silo strikes would maximize the damage done to civilians through radiation sickness, cancers and genetic damage. Calculations were that between 2 and 20 million Americans would die within the first 30 days after such an attack. A similar and additional total of deaths would result from attacks on bomber bases and submarine bases, which are nearer to centres of population. Casualties of the same order of magnitude would be produced by a similar attack on the Soviet Union.[12]

It is true to say that strategic nuclear weapons, at least, are indiscriminate of their very nature. They do not allow any real distinction of targets. It is important to remember in this connection that they do not just give a bigger bang and kill more people around any given target but leave lethal radiation effects over a very wide area for a very long time afterwards.

Similar things must be said about any future use of tactical or battlefield nuclear weapons, especially on the territory of Europe, where they are most densely deployed. A study of the consequences of a 'limited' nuclear war in West Germany made in 1971, in which only priority military targets were to be attacked by nuclear weapons, estimated a total civilian death toll of 6 to 7 million and a total military death toll of 0.4 million. It was reckoned to be a conservative estimate, low-yield weapons being used and targeting restrictions being observed. The United Nations report in which this study is quoted comments, 'the important point emerges that civilian casualties could hardly be reduced below a certain, very high level, given the collateral effects of the nuclear attacks against the enemy's air force and other long range systems. Civilian casualties would outnumber the military ones by more than 12 to 1.'[13] The best-informed commentators have insisted that any use of tactical nuclear weapons carries with it a very high risk of escalation to general war, in which distinctions between targets would be impossible.[14]

Any discussion of the possibilities of waging limited war with nuclear weapons or of making any meaningful discrimination between military and civilian targets is academic in the worst sense if it does not give full weight to these well-founded judgments.

If the conditions for arguing from the lesser of two evils which I mentioned above are accepted it seems that nuclear deterrence must be renounced on the grounds that it involves the real possibility of committing acts of great evil, namely the indiscriminate killing of non-combatants.

Now there are two standard ways of trying to avoid this conclusion. One of them runs counter to the *jus in bello* part of the Just War Doctrine in one of its major principles – that of non-combatant immunity. It denies that discrimination between combatants and non-combatants makes any moral sense in conditions of modern total war. The argument may run along these lines: total war is war to which the state commits the totality of its resources against an adversary equally engaged. In such war the non-combatant is engaged in the prosecution of the war by virtue of his citizenship; because of his citizenship he contributes to the efficacy of the combatant; he enjoys those interests which the combatant is defending. Dedicating himself to the support of the combatant, however, he forfeits his innocence, and it is innocence which is at the root of discrimination. The totality of war resides not in the exposure of the innocent to military violence but the contribution of the civilians to the war effort, a contribution which strips them of their innocence.

Three things must be said about this kind of argument: first, it is at least a moot point as to whether total war *means* that all the citizens of a state are implicated in hostilities or whether, on the contrary, it means that they are having unrestrained war made against them. The kind of argument offered above has the appearance of a rationalization, from 'capable of being attacked' to 'worthy of being attacked'. It would not be the first time in human affairs that guilt is imputed to particularly vulnerable groups of people in order to prepare the ground for attacks against them which may be necessary for other reasons. Some recent opinions on total war lead me to the conclusion that it is indeed a rationalization of this kind that is being offered by this type of argument. Thus the international lawyer, G. Schwarzenberger, has defined total war in the following way:

Total war means war conducted in such a manner that the necessities of war form the overriding test of belligerent action. If legal rules of warfare exist which set limits to the necessities of war, the doctrine and practice of total war cannot help coming into conflict with international law.[15]

In other words total war *is* war in which military necessity is put before the humanitarian considerations which are the substance of the international laws of war, including non-combatant immunity. I am inclined to accept the judgment of the moral theologian John C. Ford on the immorality of obliteration bombing in the Second World War.

Is it not evident that the most radical and significant change of all in modern warfare is not the increased co-operation of civilians behind the lines with the armed forces, but the enormously increased power of the armed forces to reach behind the lines and attack civilians indiscriminately, whether they are thus co-operating or not?[16]

Second, in whatever way innocence is to be understood when applied to non-combatants, there will always be a large proportion of the inhabitants of any modern city who are wholly innocent: most children under 14, say, mentally subnormal individuals, as well as many ordinary people whose lives are not in any relevant sense dedicated to the cause of the state to which they happen to be subject, and who are going about their normal lives in peace.

Third, the way of thinking described above betrays a radical misunderstanding of what innocence signifies in the Just War traditions as it has been developed from medieval times until the present day. It could be summed up in two propositions:

1 Non-combatant immunity is not primarily intended as a judgment of moral innocence, but as a limit to the scope of violence and destruction of human life.
2 Human beings are not (morally or legally) liable to attack because they are citizens of a nation with which one is at war, but only – if at all – because they have the function of prosecuting the war itself.

One of the main sources of the rule of non-combatant immunity was the medieval chivalric code: the duty of the strong to protect the weak and defenceless and to confine violence to those whose duty it was to engage in it for the sake of justice.[17] Another source was the ecclesiastical Peace of God, the purpose of which was to curb the violence endemic to medieval society by declaring certain classes of people immune from attack, especially clerics of all kinds and peasants cultivating the soil.[18] These traditions were eventually brought together with the originally quite separate Christian moral rule against killing the innocent to form the non-combatant immunity rule of the Just War Doctrine, on the assumption – certainly correct – that most of the people listed as immune from attack are indeed generally innocent of the injustice that is being fought against. As the modern Just War Doctrine took shape in later centuries this principle of limitation of violence to certain categories of people was maintained with remarkable consistency. It received added momentum from the rejection of war on grounds of religion by the founders of the international law tradition, Vitoria and Grotius. This represented a decisive shift away from any notion of collective guilt. It was not just to attack individuals because they held certain beliefs or denied others, which meant in effect that they could not be justly attacked because they belonged to a particular state. Thinking along such lines in our own day would lead to the conclusion that patriotism is not sufficient grounds for loss of immunity. It is, after all, something which the individual member of a modern nation-state can hardly avoid, just as the ruler's religion was something which an earlier citizen could hardly avoid. The development of the *jus in bello* tradition meant a denial of collective guilt and a shift to functional criteria for judgment of who may be attacked and who not. In Vitoria, Suarez, Grotius and Vattel and other Just War theorists it is social function which determines guilt rather than the fact of being an enemy citizen.[19] This raises awkward questions about the status of conscripts but at least we can say that genuine non-combatants have done nothing to forfeit their right not to be killed. Given that there are always many individuals who are wholly innocent of the injustice of a war and that it is inherently unjust to kill them, even in a just cause, the just way to proceed is to attack only those who give evidence of their hostile intent by bearing arms. Admittedly, 'bearing arms' in modern times means a lot more than being caught with a gun, and may be expanded to include all those involved with the operation, support and maintenance of weapons systems of great complexity. But there is no rational way of extending it to include all the citizens of a nation engaged in war, let alone all the citizens of a nation which *might be* engaged in war. The net result of the non-combatant immunity rule has been a firmly held intention on the part of moralists and legislators to limit the ravages of war to those directly engaged in it, because the end of all war must be just peace and not collective retribution or genocide. The contemporary International Laws of War concerned with the protection of civilians are formulated in a way which is entirely consistent with this interpretation.[20]

The second way of trying to avoid the conclusion I reached about the moral status of nuclear deterrence is different from the first in that it seeks to stay within the terms of the *jus in bello* doctrine. It argues that a nuclear deterrence is possible which is both moral and effective if it is based upon counter-force targeting alone and that it is not necessary to have a built-in – and always immoral – threat to move to counter-city warfare. The historical 'backdrop' for this belief is the declared counter-force bias of US nuclear strategy since secretary of defense McNamara's speech in 1962, reaffirmed in President Carter's 'Presidential Directive 59' in 1980. This was analysed by defense secretary Harold Brown as being simply a continuation of US settled policy of basing strategic deterrence on the threat to destroy, not Soviet cities, but 'the things they appear to value most – political and military control, military force, both nuclear and conventional, and the industrial capability to sustain a war'.[21] Nevertheless, the moralists who build upon such a strategy do not suppose that the deterrent effect comes solely from the threat to political and military power, but from the virtual certainty of enormous collateral destruction of civilian populations which would occur in any effective counter-force attack. Arguments for a 'moral deterrent' of this kind have surfaced many times since 1962 and they proceed in different ways to justify themselves by accepted Just War criteria. Since they all accept the principle of non-combatant immunity from direct attack, they must do this on grounds of *proportionality* – the other central criterion for justice in war. It holds that – even when non-combatant immunity is strictly observed – the collateral effects of any act of war (which could include many foreseen, if unintended, civilian deaths) must not be out of all proportion to the good being sought in the war itself. These collateral deaths must not be one of the goals of war, nor a means to the goals of war, nor a wanted effect of the action. They must be only the unintended, radically unwanted, but unavoidable side effects of some legitimate military action necessary for a successful and just conclusion of the war. And they must be proportionate.

There is clearly a strong element of relativity about this concept of proportionality. The most straightforward way of bringing it into the argument for a 'moral deterrent' is to claim that, relative to the ultimate goal of national survival, *any* necessary action would be proportionate in an extreme situation – even a counter-force attack which caused vast collateral destruction to civilians. It is argued that we might be faced with an evil of such magnitude and danger to ourselves – in an attack from the Soviet Union, say – that even the deaths of millions which would occur in a counter-force nuclear strike might be justified as not disproportionate. Therefore we are justified in threatening such a response in order to deter such an evil.[22] I will comment on this use of the proportionality criterion when I have considered other versions of the argument.

There are other versions which are more complex in that they are willing to admit that a counter-force war would very likely cause *dis*proportionate damage to non-combatants, but that this does not necessarily make the *threat* of such a war disproportionate. On the contrary, the wholly laudable intention of deterring war may be based upon shared knowledge that such disproportionate damage might occur if any such war were started.

The fullest exposition of this type of theory occurs in the writings of the moral theologian Paul Ramsey, who may be taken as representative. It is worth giving a brief account of this since something very like it is contained in other recent attempts of Christian moralists to justify a 'moral deterrent'.[23] It may be summarized in Ramsey's own words, as follows:

1 Legitimate deterrence 'is the direct effect of the unavoidable indirect effects (the collateral civil damage) of properly targeted and therefore justly intended and justly conducted

war in the nuclear age.'[24]

2 'Long before an actual war reaches the upper levels of massive nuclear bombardment of the sources of military power, the destructiveness of such warfare directed even upon legitimate targets is likely to be disproportionate to the good sought or the evil prevented by resort to arms. . . . If this be the case, then there is deterrence *at work* within the theoretically legitimate target area, because it will exert pressure upon any *rational* decision-maker to acknowledge that the principle of proportion is simply a summary of political wisdom.'[25] (My emphasis)

3 'A threat of something disproportionate is not necessarily a disproportionate threat.' It is still immoral to intend anything it would be immoral to do, but the central intention is not to wage even counter-force war, but to prevent it or – if war has begun – to enforce rational limits on hostilities: 'a threat of something that would be disproportionate, and which would exceed any of the reasonable purposes if carried out, may be proportionate, when weighed against the graver evil that is prevented by the threat. . . . Threats that would if carried out have disproportionate military utility may well have proportionate military utility so long as they are unemployed, or so long as they are employed for deterrent effect, to enforce shared limits upon actual fighting, and to keep war itself proportionate to political purposes.'[26]

This argument suffers from radical defects analysed earlier in this paper. If deterrence relied upon the threat of doing something immoral (in this case the immorality arises from gross lack of proportionality) then the only basis upon which it could be accepted would be the paradoxical one that it was the only way to avoid doing the thing itself, namely wage disproportionate nuclear war. If it were 100 per cent certain that this would be effective we would be in a genuine moral paradox, which (in the imaginary world where such things can occur) would be tolerable – indeed, unavoidable. However, we have once again to face the defects inherent in any policy in this world in which we actually live and make threats: namely, defects of political and strategic stability and defects of rationality which could put matters beyond our control. If there is a chance of the threat being called into action – because of unforeseen failures of stability and human reason – then the threat of doing something grossly disproportionate which is inherent in this 'collateral deterrence' could in fact terminate in doing something grossly dispropor-tionate. We cannot therefore dissociate ourselves from the real and present intention of responding to some possible future event with a grossly immoral action. 'Collateral deterrence' is depen-dent upon such an intention and is therefore unacceptable to morals. Its very rationale is a precise reliance upon a future willingness to go beyond the limits of proportionate force if sufficiently provoked. This is inescapable. It means that the attempt to drive a wedge between intention to transgress all moral limits and intention to deter fails once again.[27] The 'moral counter-force deterrence' theory is therefore forced back on the claim that actual use of the weapons in extremity could be proportionate, given the magnitude of the cause we would be fighting for.

Even if we leave aside the obvious thought that we cannot fight for anything with nuclear weapons, since their use by us would bring about our sure and certain annihilation (if that had not already occurred by enemy first strike), I believe it is necessary for us to accept that there could be no proportionate reason for such an action. The attempt to employ the Just War criterion of proportionality in the service of nuclear deterrence is in fact a radical abuse of it. That doctrine was formulated in a time before the enormous destructive power of nuclear weapons was ever envisaged. It therefore seemed reasonable – right up to the Second World War – that proportionate reasons could be found for fighting a war of defence with all the weapons available. But it did not envisage the annihilating and long-lasting effects of nuclear weapons. Proportionate reasons become more difficult to find as weapons become more destructive, until they become impossible to find altogether. In the interests of humanity – interests which are at the heart of all Just War Doctrine – there is a limit to calculations of relativity. There are degrees of destruction in relation to which no conceivable justifying purpose could be advanced. I would argue that there could be no proportionate reasons for using our nuclear weapons – even against enemy forces – given what we know of their vast destructive effects beyond the immediate targets and the very

great risk of escalation to all-out nuclear war. If there is virtually
no prospect of victory, or even of recovery, I do not see how talk
of proportionate reasons can have any sense. Such talk may have
a place in the world of strategic logic, but it can have no place in
the world of human interests. I am morally certain that none of
the Just War teachers of the past would have agreed that
destruction on the scale which would follow counter-force
warfare could ever be justified by a proportionate reason, not
even the prevention of a Soviet take-over, nor the previous use of
nuclear weapons against us.

For about 1,600 years in Europe the Just War Doctrine in its
different forms has been the framework for making moral
judgments about the use of violence by state authorities in the
interests of justice. When using it to make judgments we ought
constantly to recall that it presupposes a certain moral environment – a set of shared human interests and goals which are to be
served by its various rules and criteria. There have been
considerable historical changes in the moral environment, but it
is never absent altogether. Just War teaching – at its strong
moment – is usually being asserted over against some other
doctrine of war which is thought to violate the deepest interests
of humanity. Such for instance was the doctrine of crusading
religious war which flourished in the sixteenth and seventeenth
centuries and against which the great Just War teachers who are
at the origin of the modern tradition hammered out the rules of
restraint.[28] The moral environment in which the *jus in bello*
restraints ought to be employed is not one which is concerned
only with the rights of states considered as super-individuals. The
primary concern is with the rights of individual persons in
community over against the claims of military necessity. States
themselves exist for the good of human community and its
individual members in any case, and they recognize this by
recognizing customary rules and written agreements against
unrestrained killing in time of international conflict. Thus, for
instance, all the four Geneva Conventions of 1949 are concerned
in great detail with the protection of individuals who are the
victims of war: the wounded and sick members of armed forces
on land and sea, prisoners of war, and civilians who fall into
certain categories of protected persons, especially women,
children, the sick, aliens and the inhabitants of occupied

territories. Virtually all states in the world are parties to the conventions, which have the force of international law. The Conventions were much added to by the Protocols of 1977, especially Protocol I, Part IV, relating to the immunity of civilian populations from direct attack. Article 48, the Basic Rule, states:

> In order to ensure respect for and protection of the civilian population and civilian objects, the Parties to the conflict shall at all times distinguish between the civilian population and combatants and between civilian objects and military objectives and accordingly shall direct their operations only against military objectives.[29]

The article prohibiting indiscriminate attacks has already been cited on page 49 (see page 63, note 9). Any likely use of nuclear weapons such as are possessed and targeted by Britain would be forbidden by this Protocol, and would be contrary to the entire thrust of developing international law in this area. Unlike the 1949 Convention, however, the 1977 Protocol is signed but not ratified by Britain. Moreover, both Britain and the USA added reservations to the effect that 'the new rules introduced by the Protocol are not intended to have any effect on and do not regulate or prohibit the use of nuclear weapons.'[30] They could hardly say anything else – though it is to be noted that the Soviet Union preferred to keep silent on the matter. The fact that the reservations were made simply emphasizes with great clarity the complete contradiction between nuclear weapons and the Laws of War. In a very major sense, the use of nuclear weapons, and the threat to use them, flagrantly violates these laws and the moral framework within which they stand.[31]

Nuclear deterrence and the Laws of War relating to protection of civilians have been two flatly contradictory developments issuing from the barbarous conduct of nations during the Second World War. The one accepts the barbarous doctrine of total war, the other denies it. But this contradiction is not something imposed upon us by natural forces beyond our control. Both developments are the products of human choices: in the case of nuclear deterrence, a series of choices since 1945 to base defence on the acquisition of the most powerful offensive weapons within reach, regardless of moral constraints. We may be forced to the conclusion that a completely guaranteed – and at the same time, moral – defence is not possible in the nuclear age and that we have to make a choice between an immoral defence or one which would be ineffective in the face of a nuclear armed adversary. There will be those who say that such a limited defence is no defence at all, and they will not be impressed by the arguments presented in this paper, however just they are. But they should consider the truth that threats of ultimate violence are not necessarily the most effective threats and therefore not the best kind of defence. They may well be grossly counterproductive in the long term. Ultimate weapons create ultimate enemies and put everyone within 15 minutes of extermination for the forseeable future. A completely guaranteed defence is in fact an illusion created by possession of these weapons. There is no guarantee whatever that rationality – already much eroded by nuclear deterrence – will not break down altogether under stress and the weapons be sent to the very destinations on which they are now targeted. It is therefore imperative to develop an alternative defence system which can be used in a moral and a rational way.

Notes

1 See 'Nuclear Weapons and Preventing War', in *Statement on the Defence Estimates*, London, HMSO, 1981, p. 13, reprinted as a separate pamphlet by the Ministry of Defence Public Relations; also, 'The Future United Kingdom Strategic Nuclear Deterrent Force', Ministry of Defence Open Government Document, 80/23, July 1980; also, 'Preventing War' by Michael Quinlan, deputy under-secretary of state, Ministry of Defence, in *The Tablet*, 18 July 1981, and the ensuing correspondence.
2 It is discussed in detail by Barrie Paskins, 'Deep Cuts Are Morally Imperative', in Geoffrey Goodwin (ed.), *Ethics and Nuclear Deterrence*, London, Croom Helm, 1981, p. 103ff. He argues that East/West deterrence is robust, i.e. it does not depend on a delicate balance and therefore deep unilateral cuts, which would initiate a genuine disarmament process, are not only morally imperative but possible without precipitating war.
3 Some Soviet views on this matter are related in the US Congress report on *The Modernization of NATO's Long-Range Theatre Nuclear Forces*, Committee on Foreign Affairs, US House of Representatives, Government Printing Office, 1981, p. 52. Also, Lawrence Freedman, *The Evolution of Nuclear Strategy*, London, Macmillan, 1981, p. 366, note 23, confirming Soviet development towards a launch-on-warning policy.

4 For instance, Geoffrey Goodwin, Emeritus Professor of International Relations, London School of Economics, in 'Deterrence and Detente: the Political Environment' in Goodwin (ed.), *op. cit.*, pp. 33 and 34; Lord Mountbatten in a speech made in Strasbourg, 11 May 1979, reprinted by World Disarmament Campaign in association with the UNA; Dr George Kistiakowsky, former presidential scientific advisor and US Rear-Admiral Gene R. La Roque, in the *Bulletin of Atomic Scientists*, September 1979, p. 23; Sir Martin Ryle FRS, in *Towards the Nuclear Holocaust*, London, Menard Press, 1981; A.J.P. Taylor, in his 1982 Romanes Lecture at the University of Oxford, 'War in Our Time'; Lord Zuckerman, in *Nuclear Illusion and Reality*, London, Collins, 1982; Dr Frank Barnaby, ex-director of SIPRI, *The Nuclear Arms Race*, Bradford Peace Studies, no. 4, London, 1981. Even such a 'neutral' observer as Lawrence Freedman had this to say in conclusion to his comprehensive study, *op. cit.*, p. 399: 'An international order that rests upon a stability created by nuclear weapons will be the most terrible legacy with which each succeeding generation will endow the next. To believe that this can go on indefinitely without major disaster requires an optimism unjustified by any historical or political perspective.'

5 This particular point was the main burden of Lord Mountbatten's 1979 Strasbourg speech, see note 4 above.

6 See Freedman, *op. cit.*, pp. 68, 96 and 372.

7 In fact, chess is a favoured image of the nuclear deterrence apologists: see the Ministry of Defence pamphlet, 'Nuclear Weapons and Preventing War', mentioned in note 1 above.

8 A recent example of an argument which does try to find the least morally wrong course is that of Sir Arthur Hockaday, second permanent under-secretary of state, Ministry of Defence, in 'In Defence of Deterrence' in Goodwin, *op. cit.*, p. 84: 'What I am arguing is that, although the conditional intention (of using nuclear weapons in war) may contain an element of moral evil, a strategy of deterrence involving the conditional intention may be the most effective way of securing the twin objectives of preventing war and checking political aggression and may therefore be a morally acceptable price to pay to achieve those objectives.'

9 The latest definition of indiscriminate attacks occurs in the *1977 Geneva Protocol I Additional to the Geneva Conventions of 12 August 1949, and Relating to the Protection of Victims of International Armed Conflicts*, Article 51, Protection of the civilian population:

'Indiscriminate attacks are:
(a) those which are not directed at a specific military objective;
(b) those which employ a method or means of combat which cannot be directed at a specific military objective; or
(c) those which employ a method or means of combat the effects of which cannot be limited as required by this Protocol;
and consequently, in each such case, of a nature to strike military objectives and civilian object without distinction.'

Text in Adam Roberts and Richard Guelff (eds), *Documents on the Laws of War*, Oxford, Clarendon Press, 1982, pp. 415-16. It should be noted in view of the discussion on non-combatant immunity below that this definition of discrimination covers the effect of weapons rather than the intentions of those who use them. It is what the weapons do that is discriminate or indiscriminate, rather than what those who use them intend to do with them.

10 David Owen, former Labour foreign secretary, and David Greenwood of the Aberdeen Centre for Defence Studies in the Granada programme, 'World in Action', ITV, 11 January 1982. For the terms of the decision, see also Lawrence Freedman, *Britain and Nuclear Weapons*, London, Macmillan, 1980, p. 47, and 'To Moscow at a Price', in *The Economist*, 10-16 May 1980, p. 24.

11 Solly Zuckerman, *op. cit.,* pp. 53 and 69. He points out also that too much theoretical weight is usually given to the idea of missile accuracy: 'it is inevitable too, that were military installations rather than cities to become the objectives of nuclear attack, millions, even tens of millions, of civilians would nonetheless be killed, whatever the number of missile sites, airfields, armament plants, ports, and so on that would be destroyed. As I have said, statements of the accuracy of missile strikes are given in terms of the acronym CEP (circular error probable), i.e. the radius of a circle within which fifty per cent of strikes would fall. Even if one were to assume that navigational, homing and all the other devices worked perfectly, the fifty per cent outside the magic circle would not necessarily have a normal distribution; that is to say, the strikes falling off in regular fashion with increasing distance from the pre-ordained target' (p. 55).

12 *The Effects of Nuclear War*, Office of Technology Assessment, Congress of the United States, London, Croom Helm, 1980, p. 83.

13 United Nations General Assembly, 'Comprehensive Study on Nuclear Weapons, Report of the Secretary-General', 12 September 1980, p. 75. See also Lord Zuckerman's report on NATO nuclear war-games: 'The picture that emerged from a series of tests was fairly consistent. In a nuclear battle on NATO territory, between 200 and 250 nuclear "strikes" of average yield 20 kt would be exploded in the space of a few days in an area no more than 50 by 30 miles (80 by 50 km). The effect would have been indescribable, and meaningless from the point of view of any continuing battle between opposing armies', *op. cit.*, p. 64.

14 For instance President Carter's defense secretary, Mr Harold Brown, on 20 August 1980: 'We know that what might start as a supposedly controlled, limited strike could well – in my view would very likely – escalate to a full-scale nuclear war.' Reported in *Survival*, Nov./Dec. 1980, pp. 267-9. It is also extremely important for the estimation of any likely consequences of using nuclear weapons in however limited a way to begin with what Soviet spokesmen and military writers have always rejected, the possibility of a limited nuclear war. See V.D.

Sokolovsky, *Soviet Military Strategy*, ed. Harriet F. Scott, 1975, pp. 11 and 64ff. and Lt–Gen. Milshtein interviewed in *The New York Herald Tribune*, 28 August 1980, reprinted in *Survival*, Nov./Dec. 1980.

15 Georg Schwarzenberger, *International Law*, Vol. II, *The Law of Armed Conflict*, Abingdon Professional Books, 1976, p. 150.

16 John C. Ford, 'The Morality of Obliteration Bombing', in *Theological Studies*, 5 (1944), p. 281. Two years later, in a radio broadcast, he made this judgment even more concise: 'Beware of people who talk of modern war as total. It is total not because all the civilians wage it, but because all of them are its targets', quoted in Paul Ramsey, *War and the Christian Conscience*, Durham, NC, Duke University Press, 1961, p. 70. Ramsey agrees with this judgment: 'Only the erosion of the tradition of civilized or just warfare could bring it to pass that these people (non-combatants) are regarded as the justifiable targets of direct military action. . . . In this regard, the just war theory has not become inapplicable . . . it has simply not been applied. That is the measure of our barbarism, and not a factual report of the changes brought about by modern warfare in placing all the people in the position of making war' (p. 70).

17 See James Turner Johnson, *Just War Tradition and the Restraint of War*, Princeton University Press, 1981, p. 122.

18 *Ibid.*, p. 127ff.

19 See James Turner Johnson, *Ideology, Reason and the Limitation of War*, Princeton University Press, 1975, p. 196ff. Cf. the judgment of Paul Ramsey: 'The sea-change that has come about is that today people do not stand even within hailing distance of the meaning that was hammered into the terms of the just – or limited – war theory. There an "innocent" person did not mean an altogether harmless person, even militarily speaking, but one who did not participate directly, or with immediate cooperation in the violent and destructive action of the war itself', *op. cit.*, p. 72.

20 E.g., the *1949 Geneva Convention IV Relative to the Protection of Civilian Persons in Time of War* and the 1977 Protocol additional to it. The 1949 Convention was a direct response to the barbarism of civilian bombing in the Second World War. According to Roberts and Guelff, *op. cit.*, p. 388: 'the provisions of the 1949 Geneva Conventions came to be seen as embodying individual rights of protected persons.

21 Harold Brown, 'The Objective of US Strategic Forces', 20 August 1980, in *Survival* Nov./Dec. 1980.

22 Such a conclusion is at least implicit in a letter of Mr Michael Quinlan in *The Tablet*, 15 August 1981, and in Sir Arthur Hockaday, *op. cit.*

23 Notably *ibid.*, pp. 68-93.

24 Paul Ramsey, *The Just War*, New York, Scribners, 1968, p. 294.

25 Paul Ramsey, 'More Unsolicited Advice to Vatican Council II', in

Peace, the Churches and the Bomb, Council on Religion and International Affairs, New York, 1965, p. 46, reprinted in *The Just War*.

26 Ramsey, *The Just War*, pp. 304-6.
27 Cf. the incisive critique of Ramsey's arguments by Walter Stein, 'The Limits of Nuclear War: Is a Just Deterrence Strategy Possible?', in *Peace, the Churches and the Bomb*, p. 73.
28 See James Turner Johnson, *op. cit.*, for details of the divergence between the Holy War and the limited war traditions, both deriving from the classical Just War Doctrine but radically different in their emphasis.
29 In Roberts and Guelff (eds), *op. cit.*, p. 414.
30 *Ibid.*, p. 462.
31 Richard Falk, Professor of International Law at Princeton, in a lecture given in Oxford on Nuclear Weapons and International Law, 2 March 1982.

The Politics of Truth. Experts and Laypeople in the Nuclear Debate

John Krige

> Each society has its regime of truth, its 'general politics' of truth: that is, the types of discourse it harbours and causes to function as true; the mechanisms and instances which enable one to distinguish true from false statements, the way in which each is sanctioned; the techniques and procedure which are valorised for obtaining truth; the status of those who are charged with saying what counts as true.   M. Foucault[1]

The 'Soviet Threat'

The prospect of being the victim of a nuclear war is horrifying. As Khrushchev pointed out, one lesson of Hiroshima and Nagasaki is that those who are immediately pulverized by a nuclear explosion are the 'lucky' ones. Survivors close to the detonation are likely to be blinded by the flash, burnt by the heat, mutilated by the blast, and lose their hair and vomit blood due to radiation. Their physical agony will be compounded by mental anguish as they pick their way through charred rubble surrounded by the dead and dying. Nor will help and comfort necessarily be at hand. In the aftermath of the explosion medical assistance will be, at best, limited and sporadic. It will be virtually nonexistent if the country or region has been subjected to a full-scale nuclear attack. So too, for that matter, will all the other support systems of social life. An all-out nuclear war involving the superpowers will, in a very short time, bomb western 'civilization' back into the stone age. As President Nixon once remarked, 'I can go into my office and pick up the

John Krige

telephone and in twenty-five minutes seventy million people will be dead.'[2] That is probably a conservative estimate today.

It is one thing to argue that the consequences of nuclear war are so appalling that such a conflict must be avoided at all costs. It is another to decide what steps must be taken to stop it happening. Indeed there seem to be two opposed views on how best to avoid the holocaust. One, that favoured by 'the establishment', holds that we must increase and further sophisticate our nuclear arsenals to keep the peace. The other, favoured by some of its most vociferous critics, insists that the only way to avoid war is to create an international nuclear-free zone. Ironically, both positions are consistent with a genuine desire to spare humanity the trauma of another Hiroshima – though arms manufacturers and their political lobbies doubtless have rather different motives for designing new and even more lethal and hideous weapons of destruction.

On the face of it, the latter policy, the policy of international nuclear disarmament, is the safest way to avoid a holocaust. One cannot fight a nuclear war without nuclear weapons. Conversely, the very fact that such weapons are deployed, that they lie in readiness in thousands of launching pads on the earth, beneath the sea, and in the air, makes nuclear war more likely – whether by accident or by design. Surely the only way to guarantee that no one is ever Hiroshima'd again is to abolish nuclear weapons altogether.

As persuasive and self-evident as this line of reasoning may be, it constantly founders on what are taken to be the political realities of the modern world. Two assumptions in particular are central to the strategies advocated by many defence 'experts' in this country. First, it is assumed that under no circumstances can Russian-style communism be tolerated here, or indeed anywhere in the 'free' world or its satellites. Second, it is assumed that, unless deterred, the Soviet Union will colonize Europe as part of its overall strategy of achieving global domination and hegemony. To this end Russia is constantly expanding and developing its stockpile of weapons of mass destruction.

From this point of view, to disarm would be to court disaster. Security lies in strengthening the NATO alliance and in developing weapons systems so devastating in their effects that the Russians would never dare launch a nuclear offensive. It is only fear of the consequences which can curb Soviet expansionism. We must arm and rearm to ensure the survival of our society and our way of life – not disarm.

The claim that the major threat to peace lies in Soviet expansionism and its military build-up is worth scrutinizing closely because it is the one propounded by successive British governments. Typically, the UK 1980 *Statement on the Defence Estimates* sees Russia as an aggressive imperialistic power. Its leaders are determined to maintain, by force if necessary, their repressive brand of communism in Russia's European satellites. Consistent with the tenets of Marxist-Leninist philosophy, they also aim to extend their sphere of influence globally, using military means to do so if need be. They have the desire and the ability to achieve their goal of world domination: if given the chance, they will take it. It is up to the West to deter them. As far as Britain (and Europe) are concerned, 'should NATO lower its guard or falter in its determination to defend itself, the opportunities might prove too tempting' for the Soviet Union. As long as they continue to consolidate and expand their military forces with offensive capabilities, the West must ensure that it is sufficiently well armed 'that the Warsaw Pact could never count on profiting from the use of military power'.

My aim in the first part of this paper is to discuss some of the evidence marshalled by the British government in support of these claims. On the face of it, this evidence speaks unambiguously in favour of there being a 'Soviet threat' to the Western alliance. It is only when we begin to dig deeper that the picture darkens, and that the policy conclusions drawn by successive governments from the data look distinctly dubious.

This analysis is used in the second part of the paper to assess critically philosophical arguments for the cognitive authority of experts. These arguments, while suggestive, are rather limited. In particular they fail to engage seriously with the issues raised by the role of experts in what Foucault calls the politics of truth.

Is there a 'Soviet Threat' in Europe?

The size of Russia's conventional armed forces and their build-up have been taken by the NATO countries as indicating her

69

aggressive intentions. In Smith's view, they 'have helped form the basis of general attitudes in NATO countries to the USSR, and lie at the core of NATO strategy and policy planning'.[3] They must therefore be the starting point of our analysis of the Soviet threat in Europe.

Figures presented in successive British defence White Papers, by both Labour and Conservative governments, are on the face of it, very alarming. Typically the 1976 White Paper[4] showed NATO'S active military personnel outnumbered by 1.4 to 1, its main battle tanks by 2.7 to 1, its field guns by 2.5 to 1, and its tactical aircraft by 2.3 to 1. Considered in isolation these figures give the impression that the Soviet Union has a massive superiority in conventional forces in Europe. Coupled with the assumption that it seeks to conquer Western Europe if given a chance, it seems clear that to deter it NATO must spend more money on personnel and equipment before we are engulfed in a red tide.

It is important to be aware of the significance of this imbalance in conventional forces to the nuclear debate. Soviet superiority at this level has not simply been taken to indicate that effective deterrence requires that NATO build up its conventional forces. It is also used to justify the deployment of 'tactical' or 'theatre' nuclear weapons in Europe.[5] Indeed, the allied strategy in Europe as described in a government White Paper specifically makes allowance for NATO's failure to contain an attack on the conventional level. Thus it is stated that:

> The strategy is intended to deter aggression by NATO's possession of forces which are able to mount a robust conventional defence against attack, and by making clear NATO's ability and will to have recourse to nuclear weapons, should other means fail, to cause an aggressor to abandon his attack and withdraw.[6]

Not surprisingly therefore NATO, unlike the Warsaw Pact (WP), has refused to accept the 'no first use of nuclear weapons' policy, sickeningly abbreviated NOFUN by defence experts. This is all the more reason for scrutinizing the figures for conventional forces with some care. They have been presented as if they were objective, brute, incontrovertible evidence for a Soviet threat in

Europe by successive British governments. But how reliable are they? And what significance should we attach to them?

Regarding the first question, it is worth stressing that much of the data, particularly for the WP, is derived from American intelligence, and is released in reports to the US Congress, and through other channels. As such it is compiled using airborne and satellite photography, electronic spying and other techniques of gathering information.

Another invaluable source of information, particularly concerning personnel and equipment, is *The Military Balance*, published annually by the International Institute of Strategic Studies (IISS) in London. This organization derives its information primarily from a network of contacts established with Western governments, and from military attachés at London embassies. Where necessary it makes reasoned estimates to compensate for inadequacies in its data.

The dangers in these procedures are manifest. The figures that we have are only as reliable as the sources from which they are derived. On occasion these sources have been known to make serious errors. A particularly notorious blunder concerns estimates of the number of WP tanks. Initially these were made by counting the number of tank sheds revealed by aerial photography, and calculating back to the number of tanks on the assumption that the sheds were full. Only afterwards was it realized that many of the sheds were, in fact, empty!

The propaganda value of inflating, deliberately or otherwise, the number of WP tanks is obvious. On the other hand it must be remembered that the closed and secretive nature of Soviet society leaves Western analysts little option but to rely exclusively on the techniques mentioned above. Somewhat dramatically then, Smith concludes that 'even in the basic sources there is no consensus about the facts – nor can there be, for there are no "facts" as such, only estimates and approximations.'[7] These estimates are *constructed* from raw data like satellite photographs or the pronouncements of senior officials. Thus, though presented in an apparently 'objective' numerical form, they are actually the outcome of a complex decision-making process in which a variety of assumptions and value judgments are embedded.

There is no need to be dismissive about the worth of the figures derived from the mentioned sources. Lack of certainty does not justify total scepticism. Rather, one needs to proceed with caution, to be willing to revise one's estimates in the light of new information, and to recognize the uncertainty surrounding the empirical base of one's analysis when drawing conclusions from the data.

Bearing these considerations in mind, let us now focus on two aspects of the conventional arsenals in Europe – the tank forces and, more briefly, the number of military personnel.

There is no doubt that the WP countries have many more tanks than does NATO. Smith's data[8] give the respective sizes of the tank forces as 17,000 and 7,050 in 1969. By 1978 the WP had increased its number of tanks to 27,900 while NATO'S rose to 11,300. Thus the ratio of WP to NATO main battle tank forces in Europe was roughly 2.5 to 1 in 1969 and in 1978, a figure not significantly different from the 2.8 usually quoted in our defence White Papers. It should be noted, however, that although the gap in the number of tanks increased from about 10,000 to 16,600, *both* NATO and the WP increased the absolute size of their tank force levels by about 60 per cent over this period.

What is the significance of these figures? More specifically, does the numerical imbalance indicate that there is a Soviet threat to NATO? And can it be used to justify the expansion of NATO's conventional forces, and the deployment of tactical nuclear weapons in the European theatre?

Perhaps the first point to stress is that it is simply wrong to conclude that because the WP has more tanks or personnel or whatever, there is a Soviet threat to the West in Europe. Numbers alone mean very little. What also has to be assessed, first, is whether Russia has aggressive intentions in this area. As I mentioned above, this is a basic assumption made in British defence White Papers, but it should not go unchallenged. And, second, we need to know what the war fighting capability of the WP forces is. Plainly if the Soviet Union has no intention of invading Europe, or if its forces are inadequate to the task, there is no overt Soviet threat to NATO, whether or not the latter is heavily outnumbered in certain areas of weaponry.

To simplify the argument let us now focus on the war fighting capability of the WP tank force. To assess this, one has to take account of the age and quality of the equipment, its availability for launching an offensive against NATO, and the levels of morale and organization among the tank crews and their officers.

Using IISS data for 1978 we can break down WP tank forces in Europe as shown in the figure below.[9]

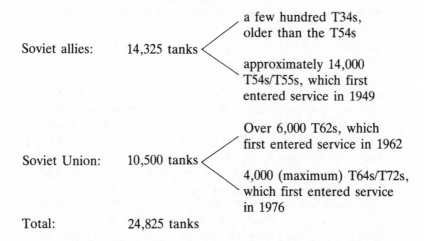

Soviet allies:	14,325 tanks	a few hundred T34s, older than the T54s
		approximately 14,000 T54s/T55s, which first entered service in 1949
Soviet Union:	10,500 tanks	Over 6,000 T62s, which first entered service in 1962
		4,000 (maximum) T64s/T72s, which first entered service in 1976
Total:	24,825 tanks	

These figures help us to put the tank gap between the NATO alliance and the WP in perspective. Clearly the majority of the tanks are rather old models. Even the T62 is merely a slightly modified version of the T54. A former NATO Head of Defence Intelligence claimed that it had the same engine as Russian tanks used in the Second World War, that its turret was cramped, and that it had to be loaded from the wrong side of the breech. As he put it, 'If they run out of left-handed midgets in the Soviet Union, they are going to be in big trouble with the T-62.'[10]

By comparison, NATO tanks are generally reckoned to be superior to the T62, let alone its predecessors. They are more reliable, they carry more ammunition, they can fire it faster, and more accurately, even while on the move, and they are better armoured. In other words about 20,000 WP tanks are obsolete by NATO standards. Although the new generation of about 4-5,000 Soviet tanks is probably superior in some respects to NATO's 11-12,000 tanks, several members of the alliance are presently developing and producing new types. For what it is worth, if we only compare the number of tanks of roughly similar age and quality, we find that NATO outnumbers the WP by about 3 to 1!

John Krige

This neatly inverts the ratio published in defence White Papers, which simply draws a quantitative comparison between the absolute magnitude of the two forces.

So much for the age and quality of the Soviet tanks. What of the morale, discipline and competence of their personnel? Would it be possible for them to launch a co-ordinated tank offensive? Considerations of this sort plainly also have a direct bearing on the war fighting capability of the tank force.

A recently published report on the military suggests that morale is deplorably low in the Soviet army. Entitled *The Liberators* and published in America, it is allegedly written by an ex-officer in the Soviet tank corps who deserted and defected to the West. Using the pseudonym Victor Suvurov the author claims that 'in many areas the army amounts almost to an undisciplined herd'.[11] Promotion through the ranks often bears no relation to military skill or experience, incompetence is rife, and ordinary soldiers sadly lack the skills to do their job efficiently. Military exercises are farcical, and are dictated by the need to put on a good show. Typically, in an exercise carried out in 1967, over 5,000 tanks efficiently and impressively crossed the Dnieper. However, the exercise had been carefully rehearsed several times before, there were tracks placed on the river bed to facilitate the crossing, and the officers had so little faith in their men that they manned the tanks themselves. The tank was too complex and the display too important to allow the lower ranks to participate.

'Suvurov' will of course tend to exaggerate the failings and to underplay the strengths of the Soviet army. His account is also rather out of date. But even if what he says is only partly true, it still constitutes a serious indictment of the army, and must raise doubts as to its ability to wage war effectively.

A different though related issue concerns the availability of all of the WP tanks in the event of a Soviet offensive. As I pointed out above, over 14,000 WP tanks, almost 60 per cent of the total, are located in Soviet satellites. One of their main uses is to maintain internal security in the Russian 'colonies' in Eastern Europe, which continually make bids for national independence. (The defiance in Hungary, Czechoslovakia and now Poland immediately spring to mind.) Strategists suspect that in the event of a NATO offensive all of these tanks would be deployed. However, some would probably be kept in reserve if the situation were reversed and the Soviet Union invaded West Germany, say. As we have seen, the tanks in question are obsolete by NATO standards, and while useful for maintaining order in a recalcitrant colony, are less valuable in the context of an East-West conflict. In short when trying to assess the number of WP tanks which would be deployed against NATO forces, one must take account of the strained relationship between the Soviet Union and her East European allies, and try to assess how they will react in response to a variety of scenarios.

So far I have concentrated on the WP force levels, only mentioning that NATO has far fewer, though more modern and more sophisticated tanks. However, simply comparing tank with tank is misleading in yet another important respect. What it ignores is that NATO has developed a vast, accurate and extremely lethal assortment of anti-tank weapons. The neutron warhead[12] is the most notorious of these, though it has not yet been deployed. In fact by late 1978 NATO had no fewer than about 193,000 anti-tank guided missiles which could be fired from ground-based launchers or from the air.[13] (The figure thus excludes short-range types which can be carried and used by individual soldiers.) If NATO continued to deploy these missiles at the same rate for a further two years, Smith estimates that by October 1980 it would have been equipped with a staggering 240,000 anti-tank guided missiles – for use against about 25,000 WP tanks!

What then is the significance of the tank gap? Tank for tank NATO is hopelessly outnumbered by the WP. But from this it emphatically does not follow that there is a threat to the alliance on the European front. For in terms of offensive capability NATO, as far as we know, is far superior to the WP. The latter's chances of launching a successful invasion of Western Europe with relatively obsolete tanks manned by undisciplined and inexperienced crews seem remote.

The gross numerical superiority of WP to NATO tanks does not necessarily imply that there is a Soviet threat to Europe. Nor does it automatically justify a further expansion of conventional weapons, let alone the deployment of tactical nuclear weapons by the West in the European theatre. These Pavlovian responses may send tingles down the spines of warmongers. They cannot be seriously considered as policy proposals for the future. After all

75

the present deployment of armaments by both sides is the outcome of specific policy decisions taken at various points in time by their respective strategic planners. Put very crudely, as far as tanks are concerned, the Soviet Union has gone for quantity, NATO for quality plus perhaps as many as a quarter of a million anti-tank weapons. Unless one wants to dismiss NATO's strategists as hopelessly incompetent, one has to accept that the Western alliance is not that vulnerable to WP tanks in Europe, and surely not so vulnerable that one has to fit anti-tank weapons with nuclear warheads.

Similar arguments apply wherever simple numerical superiority is taken to indicate a 'threat'. Consider, for example, military personnel, in which the WP outnumbers NATO by about 1.4 to 1. Propaganda notwithstanding, this ratio does not mean very much when it comes to assessing the Soviet threat. For example one has to *decide* whether to include all the troops of the Soviet Union and her East European allies. To do so without due consideration is to assume both that, for example, Hungarian and Polish troops would collaborate with Russia in the event of war, and that the Soviet Union did not need to hold back personnel to serve as 'garrison troops' in the event of an uprising in one of her 'colonies'. Similarly, as far as NATO is concerned, one has to *decide* whether to include French troops in calculations of the military balance. France is a member of NATO but her forces are not under NATO command. Thus the decision to include some or all of her troops in the alliance manpower figures rests on a political judgment as to how France will behave with respect to NATO if war breaks out. Depending on one's assumptions, quite different results are thus arrived at for the military balance in Europe, 'facts' which are produced by making hopefully reasoned, but certainly disputable political assessments.[14]

When it comes to assessing war fighting capability another set of problems arises. As I mentioned earlier, 'Suvurov' claimed that morale is low in the Russian army. In fact he goes so far as to assert that 9 out of a total of about 45 Soviet divisions 'are absolutely incapable of fighting'[15] – they are kept purely for show. Then again, it should be stressed that NATO has tended to emphasize, rather more than the WP, a policy of technological substitution. This involves reducing manpower while exploiting technological advances to enhance the ability of the individual soldier to kill and destroy. Obviously factors like these must also be taken into account when assessing the significance of troop numbers.

The insidious propaganda persists, however. The Public Relations Department of the Ministry of Defence has just issued schools with a chart allegedly illustrating the balance of forces in Europe. Bar graphs dramatically show the numerical superiority of the WP to NATO in one department after the other. The red bar for WP tanks is 2.5 times the length of the blue bar for NATO's. No indication of the quality of the forces is given. There are no bars for anti-tank missiles. At the top of the chart, inset centre, we are shown a memorial service for the war dead in Britain juxtaposed with a military parade in Red Square commemorating the Russian Revolution. Who can resist the conclusion that the peace-loving, true-blue NATO allies are threatened by an aggressive, militaristic, bloodthirsty enemy in Europe?

A rather different image of the Soviet Union emerges from the above analysis. It is that of a nation technologically inferior to the USA, encircled by a heavily armed and hostile Western alliance, struggling to maintain the allegiance of its allies in Eastern Europe, and endowed with a demoralized and undisciplined army, due no doubt in part to the bankruptcy of its domestic political system. It is such considerations which have led Neild, for example, to conclude that the Soviet Union and its allies pose no significant military threat to Britain and to Western Europe. He writes:

> The realistic interpretation of the situation seems to me to be this. The Soviet Union has developed a beastly political system through an unfortunate marriage of Tsarism and Marxism. And having acquired a European empire in the aftermath of World War II it is now an outdated imperial power facing acute difficulties in holding down its colonies. . . . The right premise from which to start is that the Soviet Union is an old fashioned imperial power on the defensive in Europe yet locked in the arms race.[16]

One may not agree with Neild's alternative analysis of the Soviet political system. But the point that I want to stress is that an appreciation of the social and political context in which both Russia and the West develop their military capabilities is crucial if one wants to identify the factors which make war more likely. Playing the numbers game may gloss Cold War rhetoric with a veneer of objectivity and value neutrality, and ensure cognitive deference to the strategic 'experts' in both camps. But it masks the values and assumptions which inform their policies, and which must be critically exposed if the world is to be a safer place to live in.

Philosophers and the Cognitive Authority of Experts

Thus far in the paper little explicit reference has been made to the role of experts in the nuclear debate. Of course, throughout my argument I have drawn on the work of experts, particularly for information regarding the military balance in Europe. However, the epistemological issues raised by reliance on them have only been hinted at. I now want to discuss some of these issues at greater length. I shall do so primarily through a critique of the arguments for deference to expert authority put forward by two philosophers, Copi and Salmon.

The relationship between experts and laypeople is essentially an unequal one. For what is an expert? Roughly, we may say that an expert is someone who has more knowledge than most in a particular area. Experts are specialists, people who have delved deeper and more extensively than the average into a specific field of knowledge. At the very least this means that they have devoted more time than is usual to study and investigation.[17] Today it also tends to mean that they have undergone a period of advanced training in a speciality and that they have access to resources not readily available to the nonspecialist.

The inequality in the distribution of knowledge between laypeople and experts means that, in certain situations, the former are *cognitively dependent* on the latter. The relationship is cognitive because it arises specifically at the level of knowledge, and concerns what one can justifiably believe to be true. It is a dependent relationship because the nonspecialist lacks the opportunity, the training and the access to resources which the expert has. At the same time, in the eyes of the layperson, the expert is a *cognitive authority*, i.e. one who is privileged to speak authoritatively in a particular field of knowledge, and to whom deference is due. It is this deference which is reflected in the uncritical acceptance of expert pronouncements by most lay-people.

In their writings on expertise, the main concern of the two logicians, Copi and Salmon, is whether or not it is rational for laypeople to defer to experts. Put differently, granted that laypeople sometimes trust experts, is their trust a matter of 'faith' or of reason? Is it legitimate for laypeople to sacrifice their intellectual autonomy to the cognitive authority of another?

Both of these writers suggest that it is indeed rational for laypeople to accept assertions on the authority of experts, at least when they fall within the expert's field of knowledge. Copi, for example, remarks that:

> the reference to an admitted authority in the special field of his competence may carry great weight and constitute relevant evidence. If laymen are disputing over some question of physical science and one appeals to the testimony of Einstein on the matter, that testimony is very relevant. Although it does not prove the point, it certainly tends to confirm it.[18]

Salmon echoes these sentiments in his discussion of experts.[19] Experts, he suggests, are typical 'reliable authorities' in their chosen subjects. One can reasonably appeal to their status as such in support of a conclusion. Like Copi, Salmon stresses that such appeals do not constitute decisive grounds for taking something to be true – even reliable authorities sometimes make mistakes. Thus for both writers, the fact that an *expert* has said something in his or her particular field of knowledge is a reason, though not a conclusive reason, for a layperson to believe that it is true.

Salmon goes beyond Copi in identifying those special characteristics by virtue of which experts are supposed to be reliable authorities. The authority, he says:

> is known to be honest and well-informed in the subject under consideration. . . . Finally, – and this is the crucial point – the expert is known to have based his judgement on objective

John Krige

evidence which could, if necessary, be examined and verified by any competent person.[20]

It is because experts have these qualities that it is reasonable to defer to them.

Having identified some of the circumstances under which it is rational to defer to experts, Salmon goes on to point out that there are times when they are not to be regarded as cognitively authoritative. For example, an expert has no special epistemic status outside his or her field of competence, as Copi also noted. Of more pertinence to our earlier argument, which involves a controversy with major political and policy overtones, Salmon points out that when apparently equally competent experts disagree, we have:

> no reason to place greater confidence in one than in the other, and people are apt to choose the authority that gives them the answer they want to hear. Ignoring the judgement of opposed authorities is a case of biasing the evidence. When authorities disagree it is time to reconsider the objective evidence upon which the authorities have supposedly based their judgements.[21]

Salmon rightly notes that when experts disagree it is all too easy to ignore the opinions and testimony of one of the protagonists. Those who do so are simply using objective-sounding statements to buttress and rationalize their own preferences, and to surround them with an aura of scientific legitimacy. On the other hand, the alternative which he suggests – that one should look again at the empirical evidence – is both naïve and limited. The implication that a dispute between experts could be settled by appealing to a more or less unproblematic empirical base is a positivistic legacy in Salmon's work which seriously underestimates and misrepresents the complex sources of disagreement between him and Copi.

One reason why experts often fail to agree is that they are actually addressing themselves to different problems.[22] Indeed, in disputes between experts a process of negotiation can occur in which the range of questions deemed relevant to a particular issue is contested, and perhaps never settled. Along with

80

judgment as to what problems should be investigated goes a decision as to what facts are relevant to the problem. Thus experts can find themselves at loggerheads about the *relevance* of evidence, and this quite apart from the question of whether or not that evidence is 'objective' and its sponsors honest and well informed.

Without wishing to imply that I am an expert in the nuclear debate, some of the arguments developed earlier in the paper can be used to illustrate this point. So, for example, I spent some time discussing the war fighting capability of WP personnel, and adduced evidence that they were inexperienced, undisciplined and low in morale. In my opinion this evidence is relevant to the question of whether or not there is a 'Soviet threat' in Europe. Yet it is omitted from many arguments for the existence of such a threat put forward by those who advocate the strengthening and extension of NATO's weaponry. A generous interpretation of this omission is that NATO's strategists do not regard such evidence as important. Alternatively, of course, they may simply be suppressing it because they find it unpalatable. But the fact remains that we have here the seeds of a dispute, not over the reliability of the evidence, but over its pertinence to the question of the 'Soviet threat'.

From an epistemological point of view, a rather more fundamental source of disagreement between experts is the intrinsic uncertainty and ambiguity surrounding so-called 'objective' evidence and its interpretation. At the risk of oversimplification, we can identify two particular levels of disagreement: first, disagreement over what the facts are and, second, disagreement over how a particular set of putative facts is to be interpreted.

Regarding the first of these, it is important to realize, *contra* Salmon's positivistic claims, that even apparently simple matters of fact can precipitate heated controversy. For example, on the face of it, the number of WP tanks or of NATO personnel available to launch an offensive in Western Europe is a straightforward matter of fact. But as we have seen this is just not so. Do we allow for the possibility that some tanks may be kept in reserve to retain order in some of the Soviet Union's discontented satellites? And can we be sure that the French will make their forces available to NATO in the event of the latter moving aggressively against the WP? These are decisions to be taken in the light of political judgments, judgments which substantially alter one's assessment of what the 'facts' are regarding the matters identified, and which can be critically challenged.

Related to this question is the one of how the facts are to be interpreted. Indeed much of the first part of this paper can be understood as involving a dispute at this level. More specifically, granted the numerical superiority of the WP to NATO in some areas of weaponry – and we can quibble about the precise ratios, but the general trend is clear – does this mean that there is a Soviet threat to the Western alliance in Europe? Against successive statements by the British government and her advisers, I have insisted that it does not, that mere weight of numbers does not signify offensive capability, and that to suggest that it does is to draw conclusions not justified by one's evidence and to engage in dangerous scaremongering and blatant propaganda.

In some respects the example I have chosen is a bad one precisely because the evidence put forward by the establishment which I have discussed is very unconvincing. Indeed it seems to be used to reinforce with 'scientific facts' the 'commonsensical' preconceptions in this country about the nature of the Soviet régime – hence its value as propaganda. The situation is usually not as transparent as this. Thus in a seminal discussion of the role of experts as advisers to policy makers Gilpin points out that:

> even though the expert may present his advice in terms of the technical *what is*, the advice may be important politically because explicit or implicit in the reported technical data are numerous non-technical assumptions concerning *what ought to be done*. These non-technical assumptions influence and sometimes determine the problems selected by the expert for emphasis, the facts he believes relevant, and the implications he may draw from the related facts for public policy.[23]

Gilpin goes on to say that the extent to which the expert's own political goals and values influence the advice given depends on a number of factors. For example, experts who are influential in the higher echelons of decision-making are more likely to play an active role in formulating political objectives, and will not simply serve as a resource providing technical information.

A similar situation can arise if the subject matter is scientifically complex and beyond the grasp of the policy maker. Under such circumstances, to make their knowledge meaningful to their audience, the experts inevitably relate it to the political objectives as they perceive them, selecting those facts they deem relevant to the problem at hand, and interpreting their significance accordingly. Here too the experts' non-technical assumptions play a role in shaping the information adduced and advice given.

Of course, it is not only non-technical assumptions which can shape the experts' presentation of empirical evidence. There is also a host of technical assumptions embedded in it. Many of these assumptions are tacit, for scientific research is a craft underpinned by a number of more or less implicit and flexible rules about what constitutes a good experiment, a reliable instrument, a plausible interpretation, and so forth.[24] It is skills like these which are brought into play when one is called upon to interpret satellite photographs or coded radio signals, for example.

The point that needs stressing is that these assumptions, both technical and non-technical, can serve as the sites for controversy and disagreement amongst experts. And whereas it may be fairly easy for the disputants to reach agreement on a set of reasonable technical assumptions underpinning the construction of empirical evidence, they may never come to agree on the relevance or significance of that evidence for policy. In other words the dispute between them may never be resolved, and almost certainly could not be resolved by their reconsidering the evidence which informs their arguments, as Salmon hopes.

That experts can and do disagree quite fundamentally has rather contradictory consequences. On the one hand it tends to undermine their cognitive authority, as Salmon points out. As such, these disputes create a space in which laypeople can regain their intellectual autonomy and make up their minds for themselves on some particularly controversial issue. Seen from this angle disputes between experts are to be welcomed. On the other hand they can also serve to engender a dismissive scepticism about the value of using empirical evidence to shape policy. In doing so, rather than fostering rational decision-making, disputes between experts can undermine it.

It is important not to fall prey to such scepticism. It is all too easy to conclude that since empirical evidence is unavoidably imbued with value judgments and assumptions of various kinds, it cannot be used to formulate rational policies for what ought to be done. Values can distort and blind; but they can also illumine. The role that they play in disputes among experts depends on a number of factors including, in a controversy like that surrounding the nuclear debate, the institutional locations and political affiliations of the protagonists. That granted, one's task is not to dismiss the possibility of objectivity out of hand. It is to try to understand the obstacles which impede it in oneself and others, and to engage in the arduous personal and political struggle to overcome them.

Of the many people who constructively critized an earlier version of this paper, I should like to single out Harry Dean, Roy Edgley and Nigel Blake for special thanks.

Notes

1 M. Foucault, 'The Political Function of the Intellectual', *Radical Philosophy*, no. 17, Summer 1977, p. 13.
2 Quoted in R. Neild, *How to Make Up Your Mind about the Bomb* (London, André Deutsch, 1981), p. 135.
3 D. Smith, *The Defence of the Realm in the 1980s* (London, Croom Helm, 1980), p. 66.
4 J. Cox, *Overkill* (Harmondsworth, Penguin, 1981), p. 112.
5 Neild, *op. cit.*, p. 27.
6 *Ibid.*, p. 5.
7 Smith, *op. cit.*, p. 68.
8 *Ibid.*, p. 72.
9 After *ibid.*, pp. 81-2.
10 Quoted in Cox, *op. cit.*, p. 113.
11 Quoted in D. Smith, 'Soviet Military Power', *ADIU Report, 4*, January/February 1982, pp. 1-4.
12 For an account of the neutron warhead and the forces which led to its production and deployment, see M. Kaldor and H. Dean, 'Tanks Versus Neutrons', *New Socialist*, no. 2, November/December 1981, pp. 52-4.
13 D. Smith, 'The European Nuclear Theatre', in E.P. Thompson and

D. Smith (eds), *Protest and Survive* (Harmondsworth, Penguin, 1980), p. 121.

14 For an illustration of alternative extreme calculations of the balance of forces in Europe, see Neild *op. cit.*, p. 15. See also *The Nuclear Numbers Game*, published by the Radical Statistics Nuclear Disarmament Group, pp. 13-15.

15 Smith, 'Soviet Military Power', p. 3.

16 Neild, *op. cit.*, pp. 9 and 14.

17 The importance of this factor emerges in an interesting context in T. Pateman, 'Authority, Liberty and the Negative Dialectics of J.S. Mill', *Radical Philosophy*, Autumn 1982.

18 I.M. Copi, *Introduction to Logic* (New York, Macmillan, 1961), pp. 61-2.

19 W.C. Salmon, *Logic* (Englewood Cliffs, Prentice Hall, 1963), section 19.

20 Salmon, *op. cit.*, p. 64. There is an ambiguity in Salmon's position. Does he mean that the objective evidence could, as a matter of fact, be examined and verified by any competent person? Or is the point a logical one about the nature of objective evidence? I have interpreted it in the second sense.

21 *Ibid.*, p. 66.

22 For valuable discussions of disputes between experts see, for example, A. Mazur, 'Disputes Between Experts', *Minerva XI* (1973), pp. 243-62; D. Nelkin, 'The Political Impact of Technical Expertise', *Social Studies of Science*, 5, (1975), pp. 35-54; D. Nelkin (ed.), *Controversy: The Politics of Technical Decisions* (London, Sage, 1979); B. Barnes, 'On the Reception of Scientific Beliefs', in B. Barnes (ed.), *Sociology of Science* (Harmondsworth, Penguin, 1972), pp. 269-91.

23 R. Gilpin, *American Scientists and Nuclear Weapons Policy* (Princeton University Press, 1962), p. 15.

24 For a discussion of science as craft, see J. Ravetz, *Scientific Knowledge and its Social Problems* (Harmondsworth, Penguin, 1971), Part II. For recent discussions of the tacit aspects of scientific knowledge, see H.M. Collins, 'The TEA Set: Tacit Knowledge and Scientific Networks', *Science Studies*, 4, (1974), pp. 165-86, and H.M. Collins, 'The Seven Sexes: A Study in the Sociology of a Phenomenon, or the Replication of Experiments in Physics', *Sociology*, 9, (1975), 205-24. See also G.D.L. Travis, 'Replicating Replication? Aspects of the Social Construction of Learning in Planarian Worms', *Social Studies of Science, 11*, (1981), pp. 11-32, and B. Harvey, 'Plausibility and the Evaluation of Knowledge: A Case Study of Experimental Quantum Mechanics', *ibid.*, pp. 95-130.

Human Survival

Kate Soper

I

If those who speak of 'civil defence' intend to suggest that measures can be taken to protect the civilian population as a whole from nuclear attack, then they are speaking nonsense. Human beings do not have the means to safeguard themselves from the effects of large numbers of hydrogen bombs. In that sense, there can be no such thing as civil defence.

It has been objected that much the same forecasts were made before the Second World War. I am more impressed by the fact that the sixteen missiles housed on one allegedly out-of-date Polaris submarine are equivalent in explosive power to all the munitions used in the last war, that there are thousands of similar weapons currently stored on earth, and that the explosions of a significant proportion of these would be concentrated within the first *hours* of any nuclear war. Nor is it merely a secondary effect of nuclear weapons (except perhaps in temporal terms) that they release huge, lethal and very long-lasting doses of radiation. To maintain, in fact, that we could devise a viable system of protection against these weapons is to fly in the face of very detailed evidence to the contrary submitted by the scientific and medical communities.[1] It is to reject the admonitions of many of the military experts and politicians who are themselves directly implicated in the arms build-up.[2] There is extensive agreement today, held across the major political divides, that not only are we incapable of protecting human beings against the effects of nuclear weapons, but that global war may lead to the extermination of all life on this planet.

However nonsensical civil defence begins to look in this perspective, it none the less exists. In the United Kingdom, it exists in the form of very detailed planning for the establishment of a wartime administration, based on a hierarchical structure of control centres at regional, sub-regional and county level. It exists in a nation-wide network of bunkers to house the officials of this administration in the event of war. It exists in the form of a series of monitoring stations and broadcasting services that, it is envisaged, should provide early warning of attack, details of fall-out levels and other 'vital' information. It exists in a series of rehearsals for doomsday, of which the largest ever to be staged in this country was to have taken place at the end of September 1982.[3] It exists also in the dissemination of a great deal of information and advice about nuclear weapons, their effects and how to deal with them. This information forms the basis of the recommendations and reassurances offered to the public, as well as of all practical official planning for the emergency of war. As might be expected, some of the data is designed for general public consumption, while some of the rest is intended to be read only by those who would be implementing wartime plans.

I want to focus on two aspects of civil defence as information which I find particularly alarming and in some ways puzzling. These are (a) disparities between Home Office data and the reality we can expect in the event of nuclear attack, and (b) the nature of the concept of 'human survival' invoked in discussion of civil defence. I believe there is a connection between these two aspects which it is important to attempt to define.

I have spoken of dispari*ties* because they are discoverable at two fairly distinct levels. In the first place there is the disparity between the advice offered to the public and the assumptions upon which official civil defence planning is based. In the second place there is the disparity between these latter, more 'realistic', assumptions and the probable consequences for this country of any large-scale nuclear bombardment.

The best known, not to say most notorious, recent offering from the government to the public is *Protect and Survive*.[4] This document does indeed admit that in the event of a sizeable nuclear attack on the United Kingdom, many of its citizens would be killed instantly by blast and fire. No sooner has attention been drawn to this unsavoury aspect of the matter, however, than it is distracted by a wealth of advice about how to protect oneself from the ensuing fall-out. The suggested precautions have been fully ridiculed for their inadequacy[5] and I shall not go into that further. I am more concerned here with the identification of ourselves as *survivors* that the pamphlet invites us to make. Given that extrapolations from official American studies[6] indicate that a moderate-sized attack would leave about 16 million short-term survivors – in other words that about 40 million would be killed immediately – this invitation is inexcusably misleading. What is worse, we are encouraged not only to regard ourselves as falling into the minority category of survivors, but also to view ourselves as coping – against severe odds, certainly, but none the less coping – with the difficulties of nuclear war. We are given to believe that there would be extensive support systems available to survivors, both in the immediate aftermath and in the long term; that some kind of civil order would reign throughout the initial 'state of nature' imposed by war; and that after that period there would be a more or less swift return to 'civil society'.[7] 'On hearing the all-clear,' we are told, 'you may resume normal activities.'

Now let us compare this with the picture that emerges from documents circulated by the Home Office to local government officials.[8] In these we discover that the Home Office thinks that a nuclear attack involving some 140 weapons could destroy 80 per cent of the country's industrial base, devastate major cities and severely damage those with populations of 25,000 or over. We discover that it expects all life-maintaining services (water and energy supplies, sewage, food distribution, medical, transport, broadcasting and other social services) to be very seriously disrupted, and quite likely to be put out of action for the foreseeable future. We find it predicting that agricultural production would come to a halt, that most livestock would be dead or dying, and that large tracts of the country would be so badly affected by radiation that it would be fatal even to venture into them.[9]

It is a picture in sharp contrast to the complacency of *Protect and Survive*. Instead of 'normal activities' the talk is of the abnormalities – food riots, 'subversion', epidemics, mass burials and so on – that we can expect in the wake of a nuclear attack.

Instead of implying extensive survival a registry of the *living* is envisaged as the only realistic means of calculating the number of dead. Instead of the provision of toys and games to while away the hours in the fall-out shelter, the concern is to institute summary powers of execution to restrain the 'disgruntled or selfish minority'.

Nevertheless – and to turn now to the second disparity – while this portrayal of Britain after the holocaust is considerably more realistic than that of *Protect and Survive*, it is quite unjustifiably rosy. There is no space here to argue this point in detail; instead I shall list some of the more important factors relevant to assessments of damage that the Home Office discounts.

In the first place there is the question of the level of attack. It is assumed by government that this would be in the region of 200 megatons. Many people fear, however, that with the installation of cruise missiles Britain will be subjected to a much more intensive pattern of bombing in the event of war, one that would cover the entire dispersal range of the missiles and create a major fire risk for most of England and Wales. The Ministry of Defence itself speaks of a 1,000 megaton attack being needed to dispose of the cruise missiles. What is of more concern than the exact scale of the attack, however, is the fact that there is a definite and very pervasive bias towards 'best case' scenarios in all official civil defence exercises.

Second, as already noted, estimates of survival rates are challenged by many scientific studies that have been made of the effects of nuclear explosions. The estimates are also based on the assumption that Britain would have received a fairly extended warning of a nuclear attack, so that we would therefore have contrived some minimal form of protection. Since to put the country on an overt war footing would be to invite pre-emptive enemy strike, this assumption seems unwarranted. Evidence also strongly suggests that the government has discounted far too much that is relevant to assessments of the effects of fall-out. The additional problem of delayed fall-out (which lasts for decades rather than weeks), is scarcely mentioned at all; nor is much attention paid to the long-term effects of the relatively high doses of radiation that many survivors of radiation disease would have received.

Let us further consider that post-attack plans presuppose the survival intact of communications systems. This again is unlikely, in view of the fact that the high-power emission (known as Electro-Magnetic Pulse or EMP), which occurs at the instant of weapon-burst, is capable of destroying any electronic system linked to anything which can serve as a collecting antenna. No one seriously disputes that high altitude explosions would be deliberate policy of both sides at war, in order to exploit EMP to greatest effect in disrupting enemy communications – with the result that it could blanket entire continents.[10]

Finally and disturbingly, there is no reference in Home Office plans to the fact that the attack on the United Kingdom – and the usual assumption in civil defence exercises is that there would be a 'one-off' attack lasting some 48 hours – is not going to take place in a vacuum, but almost certainly in the context of all-out global nuclear destruction. When reckoning our chances of recovery we must at least note such strategic horrors as 'targeting war recovery capability':

> an important objective of the assured retaliation mission should be to retard significantly the ability of the USSR to recover from a nuclear exchange and to regain the status of a 20th century military and industrial power more rapidly than the United States.[11]

We can only suspect that a similar 'objective' has been recorded in the special jargon of the Kremlin – and we must draw our own conclusions.

I acknowledge that the adherents of civil defence do not intend to suggest that we can be protected against such extremes. But they too must acknowledge the probability that any use of nuclear weapons would lead to them, and review their arguments in that light.

II

Granted that these disparities exist, how can they be accounted for? One explanation is that the apparent concern for civilian welfare displayed in *Protect and Survive*, and not in the Home Office circulars, is necessary in order to conceal from the public the true purpose of civil defence. Civil defence, it is said, is not primarily about protecting us from foreign bombs, but about protecting rulers from those they rule, in situations of extreme national emergency. The 'democratic' concern for our survival serves to conceal from us the methods of a police state.

There is much in the Home Office plans that would support such an explanation. The emphasis falls heavily on the preservation of law and order, and a disconcerting priority is given to rounding up 'subversives' and controlling food riots over tending the wounded or consoling the bereaved. This cannot, however, be the whole story. The implication that present and former governments have consciously and consistently been plotting for the preservation of a tiny *élite* who would be in a position to impose its totalitarian will on marauding bands of demented rioters seems no less absurd than the idea of the WRVC handing out jigsaws to jaded survivors.

A better answer is the more obvious one that governments have been reluctant to make public the true facts about the nature of nuclear war because they are so terrifying. This explanation, although it recognizes a degree of humanitarian concern on the part of those responsible for civil defence measures, has disturbing political implications. One must question whether governments, however laudable their motives, are ever justified in systematically misleading those on whose behalf they act. Furthermore, one is bound to suspect the motives themselves behind any government attempt to withhold the truth. The importance of honesty in this respect has been well stated in a recent work:

> Governmental advocates of Civil Defence must distinguish clearly *for the public* the humanitarian and defence policy reasons for their support of Civil Defence. If Civil Defence is part of our system of deterrence by virtue of showing that we will use our nuclear weapons if we have to, it is also part of deterrence in the sense that it is integral to the process which may lead to the use of those weapons. At least people who believe in Civil Defence, if they wish to convince us that they are not trying to make nuclear war *thinkable* and thus *acceptable* to the public, will have to *begin* by stressing the real truth of nuclear war.[12]

This is surely correct. Without this essential clarification of motives doubts must persist about the extent to which misconceptions have been encouraged, in order to prevent us questioning the wisdom of Britain's reliance on nuclear systems.

The 'self-deception' regarding nuclear war practised by officials of the Home Office seem rather harder to explain. I suspect, however, that they must be viewed in the light of a general belief-cum-hope that whatever human ingenuity can contrive, it can also accommodate, and in the end survive. Those in positions of power are just as human as the rest of us in the incapacity to believe in, and to plan for, the extermination of our species. Indeed, in so far as they view themselves as having special responsibility for the rest of us, they have a vested interest in making nuclear war seem manageable: ungovernable situations are not ones that rulers like to think can occur.

When reviewed in this light, the deceptions of civil defence planning become more understandable. We can understand, that is, that some repression of the truth about nuclear holocaust is a condition of entering into serious preparations for it. The prospect of nuclear war – of a disaster more terrible than any other that our race has yet had to face – reveals the fragility of social institutions and the narrowness of the confines within which civil authority moves. It is therefore not surprising if those whose power is sustained by those institutions and conventions should want to shut their eyes to the full reality of the cataclysm, and try to get us to shut ours too.

III

I have suggested that government faith in civil defence has to be attributed, at least in part, to a simple incapacity even to conceive of human existence without some framework of social organization and civil institutions; if this is true then one must examine the language of 'survival', in which plans for the post-holocaust world are discussed and promoted. Those who cannot begin to imagine a human world bereft of the comforting structure of socially created forms of political control ought to be the first to question the identification of 'human survival' with 'the physical survival of a number of human bodies'. In fact they are the last to do so, for what they always mean by 'survival' is 'biological survival': you count as a survivor of nuclear war if you remain physically unscathed, which is regarded as a sufficient condition for the concept to be applied to you. It is thus those who are apparently least able to make the conceptual leap into barbarism, that is demanded of any realistic thinking about a post-holocaust world, who are the most ready to invoke a reductively 'barbaric' concept of survival in order to reconcile us to the loss of civilization.

The explanation of this seeming paradox lies, I believe, in the failure of the advocates of civil defence to perceive the biologism of their approach to the understanding of human society. Oblivious of the extent to which their thinking about human survival is cast in terms of the persistence of *social* forms, they consciously construe the social dimension as if it were simply a matter of the coexistence of discrete, natural individuals. They therefore find little ' problem in discovering a post-holocaust 'society' in a collection of individuals remaining physically unimpaired.

I have referred ironically to the antithesis of 'state of nature' and 'civil society' in describing the attitude of the ideologues of civil defence, and I do in fact believe that their reasoning has something in common with that of Hobbes and Locke when they argued for a certain pattern of 'civil society' and found it confirmed in their hypotheses about our 'natural' and 'pre-social' existence.[13] The main difference lies in the temporality of the argument: Hobbes and Locke hypothesized a 'natural' state through the eyes of their contemporary social existence, unconsciously reading back into the past a present whose social features they 'naturalized'; today's advocates of civil defence project into the future a 'state of nature', or post-civilization, based on their equally mistaken conceptions of what is 'natural' in present society. Failing to recognize what is irreducibly social and non-biological about our existence *now*, these advocates produce a vision of human society after nuclear war that unknowingly assumes the continuance intact of everything that is 'civil' about existing society. Yet it would be precisely in such a situation that we would be deprived for the first time in human history of every vestige of 'civilized society' and that the reduced, biologist conception of 'survival' might for the first time acquire a genuine application – as the concept of what those who remained alive had managed to do!

It is important to expose some of the confusion at the heart of the argument in favour of civil defence because even those who assert the futility of civil defence tend to share their opponents' conception of human survival too readily, and to allow the terms of the debate to be dictated accordingly. For this reason much of the discussion about the viability of nuclear shelters and other provisions that has taken place both in the media and in public meetings organized by the peace movement has been beside the point. I have been frustrated by it in much the same way as I would be were a group of doctors to discuss the chances of survival of a comatose and severely brain-damaged patient solely in terms of the technical properties of the life-support machine. But it scarcely needs a philosopher to make points that register quite clearly in ordinary language – as, for example, when we refer to the merely 'vegetable' existence of victims of severe brain damage, or say of those who have been driven insane by their experiences that they did not 'survive' them.

Given the ordinary appreciation of the problematic status of such concepts as human needs, existence, or survival, it is surprising that arguments over civil defence have been allowed to develop in such relative disregard for it. Part of the reason is that it is quite difficult to bring out and clearly express what it is that is 'appreciated'. At the risk of oversimplifying, I would suggest that what is forgotten is this: there is a dimension of human existence which is non-physical, and therefore not reproduced organically through the reproduction of the human body. It exists, for example, in language, in culture, in social institutions of all kinds, in the family, in economic and political relations, in religion and in all the specifically human relations we have with nature itself. These relationships are not born with us in the way that our bodies are, nor do they die with our individual death – a fact which goes far, I believe, in explaining our reconciliation to individual mortality. As one writer has put it,[14] this dimension of human life exists '*ex*-centrically', in the form of a 'social patrimony' that has to be distinguished from what is transmitted as a biological *in*-heritance. Birds build nests, certainly, and ants and termites bequeath their heaps, yet it is only in the case of human beings that an objective and non-biological realm of production is established as the basis itself of their existence as a species. It is only in the case of human beings that the biological contribution to personality, to *being*, is subordinate to the role of the social contribution, and to social forms of existence. It is through the interaction with these social forms that individual human beings constitute themselves as persons, with lives worth living.

The contents of this objective mode of existence are both material and immaterial – as concrete as Chartres cathedral or as intangible as the etiquette of those who pray within it. In Britain its institutions include capitalism, the legal system, Parliament, the Church of England, and so on; in a more general and universal sense it comprises the relations and institutions whereby we reproduce ourselves materially, the systems for transmitting knowledge and skills of all kinds, and the preservation and creation of an artistic culture.

In directing attention to the complexity and richness of our objective existence, I am not suggesting that there is nothing unlovely about life, or no room for criticism of its production and modes of organization. I mean only to indicate that without the world we have created we would exist in so minimal and attenuated a form as to be reduced to a state of non-being. Nuclear war, however, will deprive us of almost all of it overnight. The world in which we would be scrabbling for existence, in the unlikely event of our surviving the horrors of blast, fire and radioactivity, is one where we would find nothing in which to recognize our former selves as being ourselves, nor any social forms of existence in which we could identify ourselves as belonging to a socialized and essentially human aggregate. In the context of the destruction of everything that supports our social and political existence, there would be no distinctively human survival. There would be survival only in the sense that some of us had not died.

It is important to relate these claims, if they are true, to current thinking on the possible use of nuclear weapons. It now seems to be accepted that military thinking has turned away from the concept of mutually assured destruction and the maintenance of deterrence based on that threat, towards the idea that nuclear weapons could be used to fight wars in defence of national sovereignty; or even used to preserve particular systems of

Kate Soper

economic and political organization and the life styles associated
with them. It is more likely to be the case, however, that it is not
military thinking that has changed but rather the level of public
awareness of this thinking. Hitherto, I believe, most people have
viewed nuclear war as apocalyptic and believed that their leaders
saw it in the same light – as unthinkable because it would be the
end of the world; there is evidence to suggest however, that this
realistic attitude was never really shared by those who make the
final decision about the use of nuclear weapons. For example, the
American administration was actively preparing for nuclear war
during the Berlin crisis of 1959; there was talk then of the need
'to hold on to Berlin at all costs, even to general war', and of the
Western allies being 'in a good position to meet what may well be
the ultimate threat'.[15] What is alarming is that such rhetoric was
thought at the time, and in many quarters still is thought, to
make complete sense, despite the fact that, if nuclear weapons
had been used, there would have been little left of Europe to
hold on to, let alone of Berlin.

At times it seems that the biggest problem is to expose the
simplest of errors. In this case the error lies in thinking that the
use of nuclear weapons is consistent with the protection of an
even minimally civilized form of life or political community. If
any number of people were to survive large-scale use of nuclear
weapons, in the sense of remaining physically unscathed, their
existence would be the most physically barbaric imaginable. All
their time and energy would have to be devoted to the
satisfaction of the most basic physical needs; in this 'struggle
against nature' their task would be immensely complicated by the
fact that nature had been 'civilized' – by massive doses of
radiation, by an enormous increase in the incidence of cancer and
by severe genetic mutations. Such survivors, one imagines, would
not be much comforted by the suggestion that their 'basic
freedoms', or their national sovereignty, had been defended.

Now let us place this picture of possible survival in the context
of the loss of the objective dimension of existence which
survivors would also have to 'survive'. It is difficult to believe the
combination would not prove terminal. For example, it seems
likely that existing stocks of essential material resources would be
exhausted before they had replenished the human resources
themselves essential for replenishing material supplies; and that

survivors, used to a complex system of social interdependence for survival, might be simply incapable of making the necessary shift to self-sufficiency. Most importantly, perhaps, the complete loss of faith in our ability to control our own lives and environment, together with the loss of belief in the value of forms of control, authority and self-discipline, would make it very unlikely that any genuinely political coexistence could be reconstructed. Moreover, I think it is questionable how many survivors would find any point in caring for themselves, in a world that had delivered the final word on the futility of human purpose. In calculating our chances of survival, we should not underestimate the blow that nuclear war would deal to the sense of human worth and self-respect, nor the effect that it would be likely to have on one's preparedness to 'build again', even if renewal were physically possible.

I do not want to speculate further on these matters, however. I do want to draw attention to the fact that it is human civilization, in its irreplaceable entirety, that is jeopardized by the continued reliance on nuclear weapons for defence; and to the fact that deterrence cannot and will not continue indefinitely to prevent their use. One cannot help but feel that those who are prepared to gamble on nuclear deterrence have failed to appreciate the nature of the stake. There is a link in values between reliance on nuclear weapons for defence and belief that we can survive their use. The disparities between claims made by advocates of civil defence and the probable consequences of nuclear war are less alarming than the impoverished conception of human existence that appears to motivate thinking about civil defence in the first place. Conversely, those who press for disarmament – and they are numbered in millions in Europe now – do not do so simply out of fear, nor even because they have informed themselves about the effects of nuclear weapons, but because they understand something crucial about the nature of human society.

Notes

1 See, for example, the report issued by the medical group at the 30th Pugwash Conference on Science and World Affairs (1981), or that of the first Congress of International Physicians for the Prevention of

Nuclear War (reported in the *Lancet*, 4 April 1981). See also bibliography given in note 6.

2 Apocalyptic warnings from (among others), Dwight Eisenhower, Henry Kissinger and officials of the Kremlin are cited in Jonathan Schell, *The Fate of the Earth*, Picador, London, 1982, p. 6.

3 This was postponed because of lack of support from local authorities.

4 Prepared under the last Labour government, this was first made available to the public in 1980.

5 For example in Philip Bolsover, *Civil Defence – the cruellest confidence trick* (London, CND, 1980) and in *Facts Against the Bomb* (Nottingham CND). More detailed assessment of the value of government recommendations is to be found in: Peter Goodwin, *Nuclear War, The Facts*, Macmillan, London, 1981, Chs. 2, 3, 4, 5, 6; and in Drs P. Rogers, M. Dando and F. Van den Dungen, *As Lambs to the Slaughter*, Arrow, London, 1981, Chs. 6, 7, 8. See also A. Tucker and J. Gleisner, *Crucible of Despair: the Effects of Nuclear War*, Menard Press, London, 1981.

6 See Peter Goodwin, *op. cit.*; cf. Drs P. Rogers, M. Dando and F. Van den Dungen, *op. cit.*, ch. 6. The official US studies are to be found in: *The Effects of Nuclear War*, 1979, Office of Technology Assessment, Congress of the United States (published by Croom Helm, London, 1980). More information is to be had in S. Glasstone and P.J. Dolan, *The Effects of Nuclear Weapons*, US Dept of Defense and Dept of Energy (published by Castle House, Tunbridge Wells, 1979).

7 This is in contrast to the rather more Rousseauesque conception encouraged by certain elements in the private shelter business – who would cast survivors in the role of noble savages who had lost their civilization only to discover their true resources as natural men and women.

8 These are circulars distributed by the Home Office over the last decade. They instruct officials on what to expect in the event of nuclear attack on Britain, and on the plans they should make for such an eventuality. They have recently been publicized in the press and the information they contain has become more generally available.

9 See Home Office circulars ES 3/1973 and ES 10/1974 – cited in Dr P. Rogers et al., *op. cit.*, pp. 160-1.

10 For a fuller account see A. Tucker and J. Gleisner, *op. cit.*, pp. 24-5.

11 See Dr P. Rogers et al., *op. cit.*, p. 175.

12 *Ibid.*, p. 171.

13 In following C.B. MacPherson here (see *The Political Theory of Possessive Individualism, Hobbes to Locke*, Oxford University Press, 1962) I do of course recognize that I am adopting a controversial interpretation of the work of Hobbes and Locke.

14 Lucien Sève, *Man in Marxist Theory*, Harvester Press, Hassocks, 1979, p. 234, cf. p. 171 ff.

15 I draw my information here from a report in the Guardian (29 March 1982) of material that had been classified for 23 years and was made public in 1982.

Morality, Scepticism and the Nuclear Arms Race

Bernard Williams

This is a subject in which it is very easy for the matter and the manner not to seem to fit one another, in which, in particular, the passionate concern it arouses seems to demand that the answers be certain. If you cannot produce answers which are certain then it looks as if you are not even doing honour to the subject. Therefore a way has to be found to reconcile the passionate concern one feels about the subject with the fact that the answers are going to be uncertain. They are uncertain both with regard to the facts – what would happen if? – and to the analysis – how should one think about it? (that is, so long as one has not forgotten about it altogether, which is our condition most of the time). Then there is an additional anxiety about individual action; even if you arrive at a clear conclusion about what your own, or the nation's, attitude to nuclear weapons should be you then have to decide what to do about that, particularly if the government seems not to agree with your assessment. That raises the issue of general political morality which I shall return to briefly at the end of the paper.

In the case of nuclear weapons, the actions and outcomes involved are not just immense, as they are in many political issues, but for many people literally unthinkable, that is, there is a resistance to even thinking about how a nuclear war might be waged. In the heyday of a certain kind of writing about nuclear strategy Herman Kahn actually entitled his book *Thinking about the Unthinkable*,[1] by which he meant the assessment of the number of megadeaths and so on that might be involved in one outcome or another of nuclear warfare. Many people feel not just that they agree or disagree with the various assessments made in

such thinking, but that in some sense such thinking ought not to go on.

Now to say that a certain course of action is morally unthinkable often, and quite properly means that it is literally unthinkable – that is that it does not occur to anybody. But in this case, the whole shape of the argument seems to demand that in thinking what to do you rehearse what somebody else might rehearse, and if they might rehearse a course of action which involves unthinkable means, then that involves you in rehearsing those unthinkable means. I am not going to discuss nuclear strategies, scenarios or numbers of megadeaths; for one thing, that is not the present subject. The point is that the way in which people find something indecent about such rehearsals can extend more broadly to a certain tone of discussing the subject at all. Many people may feel that it is a subject of such passionate moral concern and therefore of such passionate moral conviction that it is actually inappropriate to discuss it in a dry, rational or analytic tone. Some people think that the dry, rational, analytic tone is always appropriate and that if you dislike it, that just shows that you are irrational. I do not take that view. There are some occasions for which the dry, rational, analytic tone is inappropriate, and there is a well-known and correctly hostile stereotype of the philosopher as somebody who, faced with some situation of immediate and passionate human concern, proceeds to analyse it in the dry, rational tone. But in this matter, despite its vastness and the moral challenge it presents, I would suggest that that *is* the right tone to adopt.

This does not mean that one should discuss the questions in just the terms used by strategic analysts. The problem with them, however, is not so much their dispassionate tone as that there is little reason to trust their arguments, and I shall come back to that.

It is often said that nuclear weapons are immoral. I am not saying that is untrue; the question is, as philosophers always say, what does it mean? Nuclear weapons are neither moral nor immoral – they are just piles of chemicals, metals and junk. To say that they are immoral must be short for something else, for instance, that using nuclear weapons, or possessing nuclear weapons, or deploying nuclear weapons, or making them, is immoral. I want to put before you a series of moral positions that people do hold on this issue, starting with the most general and ending with the least general. I shall start with the most general position that entails that any stockpiling, possession, etc. of nuclear weapons is immoral.

Pacifists are committed to certain views about nuclear as about all other weapons, and as far as these remarks go, they will find that their position is untouched. I shall not here advance arguments for or against pacifism, but I will make one suggestion: that, if held as an absolute and abstract position of principle, pacifism arguably entails anarchism. Absolute pacifism rests on the view that no state should ever use violence against another state, even in self-defence or in defence of others; alternatively and even more radically, no person should ever use violence on any other person, even in self-defence or in defence of others. It follows from either of these positions that no state should ever use violence on any person. But if the state is not permitted to use violence on any person then there is no state, because a state necessarily has a monopoly of violence which it can legitimately deploy against persons. From this it follows that a pacifist is an anarchist.

In practice a pacifist need not maintain such an absolute and abstract moral position. He or she might hold, for instance, that a state *is* justified in using violence if it has a just cause, but that as a matter of fact no war ever embodies a just cause. In that case he would be a pacifist without being an anarchist. Or second, he may think that the means available to states to fight their wars are such that in every way the outcome will always be worse than the cause of the war, or will violate rights in some unavoidable way. Or last, he may hold that while that is not always true, it is true under modern conditions. Modern weapons, and the nature of the modern world, are such that there is no way in which a state can justly fight a just war; if you then hold that a state should only fight a war when it can be justified as a just war then you would conclude that no modern state ought to fight any war. That is the view that pacifism is the only moral position under present moral conditions, a view that is difficult to hold without going into quite a deep analysis of modern conditions, of what the effect of present technology on warfare is, and so on. And then I think you will have come quite a long way from a purely absolute and abstract pacifism, the position which seems to me to entail anarchism.

Bernard Williams

Let me now turn from the view that all wars and all weapons are necessarily immoral to the narrower view that there are moral limitations on the methods and ends of war and they cannot be observed in the case of nuclear weapons, whatever may remain possible in the case of conventional weapons. A lot of people hold this position and I agree that some version of it is plausible. According to the just war doctrine, there are limitations on *what* wars can properly be fought, and also on *how* they may be fought. Some limits upon the conduct of war have been written into various kinds of conventions and laws, such as the Geneva Convention. Michael Walzer, in his valuable book *Just and Unjust Wars*,[2] points out that adoption of any kind of just war doctrine involves the rejection of what one might call Sherman's simplifier. During the American Civil War, General Sherman made his way through the Southern states burning and razing places to the ground, about which some people – possibly sufferers from the treatment, or some of the more squeamish Yankees – complained. To these he simply replied 'War is hell.' Sherman's simplifier means that war is hell anyway and that once you are involved, it makes no difference what you do. The doctrine of the just conduct of a war stands opposed to that; it says that it is not the case that the moment war is joined all ethical considerations are forgotten. On the contrary, it expects some conditions regulating what is done to be observed – for example, it forbids the arbitrary killing of non-combatants.

One argument for having laws of war is pretty obvious; it is that once war is engaged there should be some restriction on the things that can happen – the war has to be directed against combatants and not civilians, for instance. One argument against having laws of war, apart from the straight Sherman argument ('let's get it over with and do it as ruthlessly as possible in order to get it over with'), is that they actually confuse the issue. Being extremely vague and nebulous, they make everybody behave as badly as they would have done anyway and get a bad conscience into the bargain, they lead to much subsequent prosecution and conflict, and so on. There is certainly something to be said on both sides, but I do not want to go into the issue other than to make one purely historical speculation, which is worth entertaining in relation to the present problem.

If you ask the historical/sociological question 'When have the laws of war been observed?' the answer is obviously 'Not always.' It is not a specially modern vice that the laws of war are violated. There is some tendency to think that they were observed more conscientiously by *élite* combatants who were fighting other élite combatants (knights fighting knights, for instance) than by mass combatants, who were just going through a territory trying to feed themselves. The brutal and licentious soldiery were extremely uninterested in the ethics of war, partly for the reason that they had to feed themselves from the countryside. Technological developments in the modern world, because they include the invention of weapons of mass destruction, have made it much harder to observe and support any doctrine of just methods of warfare.

The Second World War illustrates the difficulty of honouring both the just war doctrine about the objectives of war and the just war doctrine about the methods of war. The more justified a war may seem to be with regard to objectives, the more uncompromising to the enemy may be the methods that appear to be sanctioned. Since Nazism was an enemy that anybody except an absolute pacifist would have felt justified in going to war against, the methods that were thought appropriate to employ to bring that war to an end, to win it, were obviously broader than might have seemed appropriate in a war simply of territorial defence or something of that kind.

The next argument to consider is whether the use of nuclear weapons, by their inherent nature, violates any of the doctrines about just methods of warfare. In some sense that must be the case. I shall oversimplify here by treating nuclear weapons not only as weapons of mass destruction, but as these compounded by carcinogenic effects, by radiation genetic effects and by other horrors. There may be some nuclear weapons of very limited explosive power and very low radiation effects, which barely have these ancillary effects and are not weapons of mass destruction. To the extent that that is true, the category of nuclear weapons will be a purely technical one and there will be no special moral issue about them; they will be just another way of producing explosions. But they will not be the only kind of nuclear weapon; and it is overwhelmingly probable that in practice nuclear weapons are going to be weapons of mass destruction. There is no effective way of limiting the use of nuclear weapons to small-scale, tactical, theatre or similar weapons; in fact their use would almost certainly escalate to the use of weapons of mass destruction. I agree with the late Lord Mountbatten, Lord Zuckerman and others, that the idea of fighting a limited nuclear war is an illusion. The nuclear threshold seems to be as important strategically as psychologically.

If you think, then, that nuclear weapons are, by their nature or by their effects, weapons of mass destruction, it would seem to follow that they should not be used, in accordance with restrictions embodied in virtually any conceivable laws of war. Consider, for instance, the definition of a war crime given at the Nuremburg trials: 'violations of the law or customs of war . . . such violation shall include but not be limited to murder, ill-treatment or deportation to slave labour . . . killing of hostages, plunder of public property, wanton destruction of cities, towns or villages or devastation not justified by military necessity'. There has been a great deal of legal discussion of this text because of the get-out contained in the phrase 'not justified by military necessity'. It is clearly not hard for those justifying murder, wanton destruction of cities, devastation, etc. to claim military necessity. Indeed, the saturation bombing of German cities by Bomber Command during the Second World War, at least up to about 1943, has been justified by appeal to military necessity – though it remains difficult to excuse thereafter and certainly not the bombing of Dresden in 1945.

But if there were a military necessity now that justified the use of strategic nuclear weapons of mass destruction, it would seem that this clause of the Nuremburg definition of a war crime becomes of no effect whatsoever. Roughly, if you can justify that, you can justify anything. Now if we agree about that, then at least the following would also be true. First, that a nuclear attack would be not only an incalculable human disaster but in some sense an incalculable moral disaster; and second, that wantonly unleashing such a war or attack would be a great crime (even if not technically a 'war crime'). If we further agree about that, how much follows from it? In answering that I am moving to the absolutely crucial part of the argument, to where the moral weight really rests, and I want to suggest two separate and independent points that do *not* follow from it.

The first is that it does not follow that there are no

circumstances that would warrant unleashing a nuclear attack. It is not obvious, in other words, that you can do without a get-out clause about military necessity. The second point, more relevant for our general argument, is that it does not follow from the fact that unleashing a nuclear war would be a great crime that threatening, under certain circumstances, to unleash it would be a great crime, or even a crime at all.

First, however, let me explain how there could be circumstances that would warrant unleashing a nuclear attack. It seems to me that there is a perfectly plausible argument that if a country were in fact faced with a clear, immediate and realistic intention by another aggressive power to destroy everybody in that country, for instance by nuclear means, then its government would be justified in using a nuclear attack to prevent it happening. In such a case, namely where at least one population or large set of persons is going to be destroyed anyway and the other lot are the aggressors, a nuclear retaliation could be appropriate. You may say that this is an unrealistic situation. It is not the situation that obtains between the great powers, but it could obtain between other powers.

My first case, then, is that a state could be justified by military necessity in actually using a nuclear weapon, but, of course, it is a very extreme case. A more immediate question is: does it follow from the wickedness of wantonly launching a nuclear war that it must be wrong to threaten this under certain circumstances? Is even mere nuclear deterrence wrong? There are two arguments that are supposed to show that it would be.

The less well known of them comes from the American theologian Paul Ramsey,[3] who argues that the policy of deterrence involves an immoral use of innocent parties. He says that, morally, it is like reducing the number of automobile accidents by making every driver carry a baby on the bumper of his car. It seems almost certainly true that if you made every driver carry a baby on the bumper of his car there would be fewer automobile accidents (for a while, anyway). However, it would not be regarded by most people as a legitimate way of reducing car accidents, one thing being that it is an immoral use of babies. The deterrent strategy, Ramsey suggests, is just like that. He is well answered by Walzer,[4] when he says that it depends on whether you are using the innocent population in a way that makes a difference to its members when they are being so used, or in a way that makes no difference. Being used in a policy of nuclear deterrence makes no difference to the citizens at all; all that is happening to them is that they are not having a nuclear war. Being used in the way described by Ramsey to end automobile accidents does make rather a difference to a baby, since there is a huge difference between being fixed to the bumper of a car and not being fixed to the bumper of a car. Moreover, if deterrence theory is correct, the populace is at less risk than it would be without the policy of deterrence. Therefore I agree with Walzer that the Ramsey argument does not convince.

The second argument is much simpler and more basic, namely that any threat of this kind which is inherent in the policy of deterrence must involve credibility, which means that in making the threat you must actually have the intention of carrying it out. Unlike some people, I do think that credibility involves a genuine hypothetical intention, that the deterrence strategy involves there being people who actually do intend to let off nuclear weapons if the conditions of the threat are met. But, people ask, 'can it in fact be credible? Let us suppose that there has been a first strike or some other attack. You are left with the possibility of pushing this button and releasing weapons against the other side. Would you do that? And if you wouldn't do that, doesn't everybody know you wouldn't do it?' Well, the answer to that is that *you* would not do it – that is, the morally anxious would not – but then the people who are running this strategy will not put you in charge of the button. They will put somebody else in charge of the button who will not have that view, and they would not be running this strategy unless they did. Of course, it may well be the case that if there was a first strike from the other side and there was then a pause for reflection, it might come about that the strategy was abandoned through some change of power – what enemies would call collapse of morale but others would say was a certain moral revulsion from the whole thing. That might well be the case, but what certainly is not the case is that you can build that option into the strategy itself. The strategy itself cannot be constructed in such a way that it would be abandoned at the point at which it has to be implemented. It is certainly true that the strategy itself has to involve there being people who actually do have this hypothetical intention. The question is not whether you can pretend to have it, but rather: is having that hypothetical intention itself as evil a thing as wantonly unleashing a nuclear war? To which my answer is: no, it is not.

The fundamental argument against the morality of deterrence in terms of its intentions must, I suppose, be this: if we are justified in intending to let off nuclear weapons if attacked, then it must be the case that if we were attacked, we would then be justified in letting off nuclear weapons. So if we would not be so justified, we cannot be justified in having the hypothetical intention which is essential to deterrence.

If this argument is supposed to hold purely *a priori* and to deliver its conclusion without any extra information at all, it is very hard to accept. Suppose it were *certain* that a threat involving a hypothetical intention to do something dreadful would be sufficient to stop some appalling outcome, so that it would be, in addition, unnecessary to carry out that threat. It would then indeed be hard to believe that the morality of the threat was no better than that of a categorical intention to do the dreadful act. If so, then it is hard to accept purely in the abstract the principle of the argument against deterrence. It may be said that certainty, but only certainty, would make a difference; and that no certainty, with regard to nuclear deterrence, is to be had. It is certainly true that there is no certainty; but can it be only certainty that makes the difference? If there were a very high probability that such a threat would prevent the outcome . . . ? I doubt that, even apart from imaginary cases of certainty, one can convincingly support the argument about intention purely in the abstract.

In fact, people who use the argument often seem not to think that it does work purely in the abstract. Rather, they start to bring in various considerations about Russian intentions, about American crimes, about how tolerable conditions under communism are, and so on, which do show that other considerations make a difference. And if other considerations do make a difference, then the very short argument about the morality of deterrence cannot be as good as it looks. Because that argument either settles the question very quickly, or it does not settle it at all. I think that it does not settle it.

There is one particular thing, moreover, which it crucially

leaves out. It makes it sound as though the issue might as well be whether we should bring nuclear weapons into existence. But it is absolutely central to the discussion that this is actually and already a world of nuclear weapons. The questions are not about introducing nuclear weapons, but about how to live with them granted that they do exist.

The slogan of CND in the old days, 'Ban the Bomb' – a slogan heard less in present discussions – was always an absurd slogan. It was an absurd slogan because the question arises, to whom was it supposed to be addressed? If there were one agency which could do something called banning the bomb then the problem would not exist or at least the problem would not be what it is.

Of course one thing that used to help the CND argument along at this point was the idea that we could set an example – that if we got rid of our bomb, then other nuclear powers would be so moved and humbled by this act that they would do the same. That belief has never seemed to me to be either moral or rational – it is just superstitious. We seem to hear less of it now than we did twenty years ago; I suppose because by now people generally have got less inflated and self-satisfied ideas about Britain's importance.

I do not even think that once nuclear weapons have been invented, we *want* a situation in which everyone has given them up – unless of course everyone has also given up all their quarrels as well. People talk as though giving up nuclear weapons would mean that they no longer existed. But that is a dangerous illusion. If everybody gave up nuclear weapons, and if the verification was such that everybody could know that everybody had given them up, it would still be true that if war broke out everybody would start making them again. If everybody gave up nuclear weapons, you would not go back to a situation before nuclear weapons were invented: you would rather get a situation where nuclear weapons were always just about to be invented. The level of security you could achieve with that would be pretty low. As soon as there was an outbreak of hostilities then in fact there would be a race to reconstruct nuclear weapons and that would be so unnerving that pre-emptive action almost certainly could not be avoided.

The world would be safer if there were not any nuclear weapons: of course it would be safer, but it does not follow that everyone ought to get rid of nuclear weapons. It would be nicer if they had never been invented but once the power to make them exists, it is probably better for the powers to have them and to have some idea of what they have each got, rather than waiting to see how quickly and under what circumstances they might be constructed.

The effect of all this seems to me to be that the moral arguments do not finish anything off. In fact, I doubt that the issue of the possession or non-possession of nuclear weapons is in itself a moral issue, as people go on saying, except for the basic moral issue of how to stop millions of people getting killed and civilization being destroyed. The morality of deterrence is legitimately one in which you think principally about those steps which make it less likely that the weapons get used, rather than just making an absolute refusal ever to use them yourself, and the moral approach in my view cannot avoid complex arguments about what the world is actually like.

The problem with our policies of deterrence is not basically that they are immoral. If, however, we could get a firm hold on practical and rational arguments on these questions, it would almost certainly turn out that our present defence policies are highly irrational. The trouble is, however, that it is at least as difficult to get a firm hold on the rational arguments; and if the moral considerations do not solve anything much, other arguments of political and practical rationality themselves seem to have become almost impossible to handle. That is no doubt one reason why people who are concerned about nuclear weapons often prefer to take what one might call the high road of morality. They feel terror and revulsion about the whole thing; they sense that the strategic arguments will lead them further into the bog, and they find those arguments both inconclusive and themselves, in a way, revolting.

There are at least three reasons why it has become so difficult to talk about these things in political and strategic terms. One of those reasons is secrecy. The person in the street is not provided and cannot be provided with relevant pieces of information because the other side must not know certain things, for instance about how much we know. The politics of deterrence require that each side should know quite a bit about what the other side knows, but it should not know everything that the other side knows. So you cannot inform the public at large about things that are certainly true. That is the deceit of one power by another, and hence the deceit of the people by the government. The second issue is the deceit of everybody by the military. Both the USA and the Soviet Union have far more nuclear and other weapons than they possibly can need – partly because the military on both sides pretend to their governments that they need further weapons and defence systems which they do not need but which are generated by the momentum of their own activities.

The third reason why thinking in rational terms about nuclear strategy has become almost impossible is in some ways the most baffling reason of all. This is the fact that strategic reasoning has now become so complex that it has fundamentally broken down. The essence of deterrence is that each side should replicate the other side's strategic and tactical thinking. Each side tries to think out what the other would think in various situations. Now once it gets beyond a certain level of complexity – and when, moreover, it is known that these people are not perfectly rational, are not perfectly informed, that they are acting in a panic, that they are acting under political pressures, that they are acting under pressure from the military – when that is so, there is no assurance whatsoever which pattern of strategic or tactical thinking they will in fact go through. Therefore the whole thing breaks down. One result is that the ordinary person cannot form any rational conclusions on the basis of these immensely complex arguments about what would happen if. . . .

What conclusions can we draw from all that? One possible conclusion is very pessimistic indeed – that neither ordinary people nor governments themselves have much idea what is going on, and that no one has any real notion of what it is rational to do. There are times when that is what it looks like to me.

If the moral approach gives up before it solves anything, and strategic thinking tends to collapse into increasingly unbelievable complexity – is there any more positive conclusion at all we can draw?

It does look to me as though we have to give up hoping for any really watertight arguments in this field and we had better see what we can do with some bits and pieces that we do have.

There are, after all, some things we know. One is that the more powers that are engaged in this game, the more complex the game is, and therefore the more unstable it is likely to be, the greater the risk, and that is why everyone – or at least everyone who has nuclear weapons – is against proliferation. A second thing we know is that whatever else is the case nuclear weapons cost an immense amount of money, they detract from other forms of weapon for which we know we have a use, and from other worthwhile expenditure; and in Britain's case they sustain an illusion of independence which is largely false. Moreover, it is rational to look for policies which require simpler assumptions than other policies require. Strategic arguments which are used to justify various courses of action depend upon elaborate scenarios about possible ways in which nuclear exchanges might go, scenarios about which we know just one thing – that it is absolutely certain that real life would not be like that. It will be replied that you have to use some scenario about international relations and military reactions in order to make any of these ideas coherent at all. That is right, but some policies depend more than others on getting it right under some elaborate scenario, and you know that under some scenarios you will never get it right. Therefore choose the policy that does not put so much weight on elaborate and indeterminate scenarios.

It is important here that we can be reasonably supposed to have some room for manoeuvre. The situation we have now is often represented as one into which both parties are locked in such a way that neither of them could dismantle their nuclear preparedness without putting itself at risk with regard to the other. That is, we have what is called technically in games theory a 'Prisoners' Dilemma', in which neither side dares go for the better option because they will put themselves at the risk of incurring the worst of all options. So they both end up with the second best option. I agree with those who deny that this is any longer a correct description of the situation (see, for example, Nicholas Measor's paper in *Dangers of Deterrence*[5]); on both sides, if they are pursuing a merely deterrent strategy, there are degrees of nuclear disarmament that they could embark on without putting themselves in such jeopardy. This follows from the overweight of forces to which I referred. To each side, however, it can easily come to look as though they are in a Prisoners' Dilemma.

At the margin, that is at the point at which a given change is proposed, it can look as if one is in a Prisoners' Dilemma because one is making the comparison simply from the point just reached, and neglecting the fact that, if the time span is enlarged, one could go back a bit without jeopardizing the position. Also at the margin, it seems to various generals, technologists and senators with employment problems, as if it is always a good idea to have the next nuclear device; indeed, as Zuckerman and others have admirably pointed out, there is a very short path from the argument which says it is too early to rule out a certain technical development in nuclear warfare to the point at which it is too late to cancel a certain technical development in nuclear warfare. (A special variant on this is a weapon-system – the MX missile – which at the time of writing cannot be deployed in any acceptable way.) There is in fact quite a lot of elbow room, but the rhetoric of experts, technologists and others has the effect of making it look tighter than it is.

It is out of such considerations, and a few more, that I would hope to find good enough reasons for Britain to give up its own nuclear weapons, and for NATO to undo the latest escalation on the Western side, the stationing in Western Europe of cruise and Pershing missiles. We would be declining to engage in this exercise, not because it is immoral to engage in any exercise of that sort, not because we had arrived at an absolutely watertight strategic argument to the effect that things will be safer if we get out of it. It would simply be because, in the situation of complexity, and instability, and absurdly escalating armaments which now obtain, there are at least some good and clear arguments for getting out and hardly any good and clear arguments for staying in. Well, it would certainly be a very risky strategy. But all strategies are risky, including that of going on doing what we are doing – particularly since that never consists of just going on doing what we are doing, but rather of doing new things in new circumstances.

If one thinks about these questions in the way I recommend, one that lays less stress on the morality of it all, it has the important advantage that there will not be any moral problem about relying on somebody else's nuclear weapons. One great weakness of the purely moral argument against having nuclear weapons is that it must be morally wrong to be protected by someone else's nuclear weapons: if what you think is that they are absolutely intolerable, then you must not rely on anyone else threatening to use them either. On a less moralistic way of looking at it, that is not the shape of the argument at all. It may just be a more rational strategy for us to stop having such weapons but to rely in so far as we can on someone else defending us with the nuclear weapons which I have already said that they should not all give up.

One will be met with complicated arguments to the opposite effect. You always are, whatever argument you advance on this question, and that is why I am suggesting that we should try to get scepticism about the arguments to do some work for us.

The idea that scepticism should do some work may seem impossible, an example of trying to get something for nothing. But it is not. For one thing, there are indeed some good and clear arguments for changing our policies with regard to nuclear weapons, and for thinking our present policies very dangerous. There are many and complex arguments to the opposite effect, which are met in turn by further complex and uncertain arguments. In circumstances of that kind, it is a rational policy to cut through the complex and collectively unconvincing arguments and to follow the simpler and clearer. You cannot get something for nothing in the sense of conjuring certainty out of uncertainty. The conclusion will still be uncertain, as any will be. But if there are a few simple and clear arguments on this side, and fewer or none on the other, then in a sense we will have as much reason, if not as many reasons, on our side as one can have.

There is a higher-order folly of trusting complex and incredible scenarios, and that can be denounced by getting off on one side rather than the other, on the side of the few simple and clear arguments. Moreover, granted what is at stake, that seems not only sensible but decent. To follow incredible and over-sophisticated arguments is a bad idea anyway, but to follow them *into* greater nuclear involvement must surely be worse, just in itself, than to get out of those arguments in the opposite direction.

At this level, there is another kind of moral involvement. Basically, it is simply the morality that I mentioned before, of trying to avoid the ultimate disaster of nuclear war. The commitment to that end certainly, in my view, involves looking as responsibly as one can at the actual situation, and not cutting off the enquiry at the beginning by a mere dissociation from policies of deterrence. But if such an enquiry reveals the kind of situation that I feel it reveals, then the moral commitment against nuclear war may link up with a rational commitment against expecting too much of the arguments about a nuclear war, whether moral or strategic.

Notes

Editor's note

Some paragraphs in this paper are reprinted from Professor Williams's article 'How to think sceptically about the bomb', *New Society*, 18 November 1982, pp. 88-90.

1 Herman Kahn, *Thinking about the Unthinkable*, New York, Avon, 1969 (first published 1962).
2 Michael Walzer, *Just and Unjust Wars: A Moral Argument with Historical Illustrations*, Harmondsworth, Penguin, 1980.
3 Paul Ramsey, *The Just War: Force and Political Responsibility*, New York, Scribners, 1968. Cited in Walzer, *op. cit.*, p. 270.
4 Walzer, *op. cit.*, pp. 271-2.
5 Nicholas Measor, 'Games Theory and the Nuclear Arms Race', in *Dangers of Deterrence*, ed. Nigel Blake and Kay Pole, London, Routledge & Kegan Paul, 1983, pp. 132-56.

Morality and Survival in the Nuclear Age

Susan Khin Zaw

I

Most people feel that the existence of nuclear weapons confronts us with some kind of moral difficulty or dilemma, or that their advent on the scene has somehow made a moral difference. I believe that this feeling is right, that nuclear weapons have changed our moral world, but that we do not yet have a very clear perception of this change. Consequently attempts to grapple with the moral issues raised by nuclear weapons often misidentify the issues and thus seem academic and unsatisfying. This paper attempts to redescribe the change in our moral world in a way which will allow moral concerns to take their proper place and have their proper weight in the political and strategic debate.

What then are the current areas of moral disagreement about nuclear weapons, and in what way is the discussion in these areas unsatisfying? The first thing to note is that there is at least some *agreement*: most seem to agree that total nuclear war would be a moral catastrophe, i.e. it would certainly be a terrible moral wrong if both superpowers actually did fire off all their existing nuclear weapons. However there is considerable debate about the morality of:

(a) deterrence, i.e. *threatening* and/or *intending* to launch a full-scale nuclear attack;
(b) *limited* nuclear war between the superpowers, as envisaged in 'flexible response' scenarios;
(c) use of nuclear weapons on a small (virtually 'one-off') scale by small powers in the settlement of local differences.

Even in relation to these areas of debate, though, there is some measure of agreement. It is generally agreed that discussing (b) and (c) in isolation *is* somewhat academic, since both cases carry a high risk of escalation to all-out world nuclear war. Still, are there any special moral problems associated with 'flexible response' itself? Well, the point of flexible response must be to make limited nuclear war at least *possible*; and given that a state of limited war exists, it would clearly be right for the superpowers to seek to avoid escalation rather than to invite it. Now, if the best chance of this lay in making sure in advance that no limited nuclear exchange took place on the nuclear superpowers' own territories, then the moral obligation of doing one's best to avert the moral catastrophe of *total* holocaust might seem to make it a moral requirement that they should find somewhere other than their own territories to fight the limited nuclear wars which flexible response make possible. But clearly a nuclear war 'limited' to, say, the European theatre would almost certainly end up as a 'total' war as far as Europe was concerned (that is, Europe could expect to be totally destroyed as a human habitat), and if the superpowers actually did thus destroy some other part of the world in pursuit of their own policy objectives, few would deny that they would be doing a terrible moral wrong. Yet it seems that accepting the possibility of doing this terrible wrong, and indeed intending to do it and threatening to do it if the need arose, would be part of a flexible response capability which took the risk of escalation seriously, and might even be morally required of it. This version of flexible response thus raises the same moral problem as deterrence: namely, can it be right to threaten or intend to do something acknowledged to be terribly wrong, even for the sake of avoiding actually having to do it? Europeans may feel themselves caught in a special moral dilemma, however. Concern for the welfare of humanity at large plus acceptance of the theory of 'flexible response' strategy might lead them to wonder if they should, perhaps, accept the sacrificial role for which geography as much as anything else nominates them; yet it is impossible for any European to avoid feeling that if the superpowers wish to dice with death, it should be with their own death in their own back-yard, not with anybody else's. How does this claim – which seems transparently just – bear on the strategic issue? Does or should it bear on the strategic issue at all? Does justice *matter* in the face of strategy for world survival?

Though case (c), the case of small-scale nuclear strikes between minor powers, is somewhat different, it too raises this last question. The risks of escalation there come from the major powers getting in on the act, and are therefore, while perhaps foreseeable by the minor powers, largely beyond any possibility of their control. Let us suppose that for one small country to drop one small nuclear bomb is in certain circumstances morally justifiable, and that secure in this knowledge it does so, but that the actual consequence of its doing so is Armageddon. Arguing along familiar moral lines, one might say that since the bombing country neither intended Armageddon, nor used the risk of it as an instrument of policy, nor had any control over its eruption, it could not be held morally responsible for it, nor would it be obliged to take the possible consequences of its action into account when considering the morality of its various options. One might even argue that it would be *wrong* for the government of that country to forego its nuclear option and thereby virtually commit national suicide for the sake of avoiding the risk of the general holocaust: for the duty of governments is to mind their own country's business first and foremost.

It seems to me that arguments like the ones I have just sketched invite scepticism about the relevance of morality in discussions of nuclear policy. What does it matter if threatening and intending the destruction of half the world is morally wrong, if doing so is the only way to avoid actually destroying the whole, or even half, the world? What does it matter if dropping one small bomb is morally justified if the foreseeable, though unintended, result of it is that the whole world is destroyed? There is of course a practical debate over whether deterrence *is*, in fact, the most likely way of preventing total destruction; but let us leave that aside for the moment and assume that it is. The movements like CND which seek to alert citizens to the realities of nuclear war and inspire fear and moral horror at the prospect will be positively dangerous; for if the fear and moral horror became widespread, this might in democratic countries bring about irresistible political pressure for some policy which undermined deterrence and thus made nuclear war more rather than less likely. But then urging the immorality of nuclear war for the sake of avoiding it is irrational: since it makes *more* likely the outcome which the moralists seek to avoid. Concern with morality of nuclear policy is thus associated with irrationality. This is often also linked with a further charge that moral claims are themselves essentially irrational, being merely expressions of personal predilections or emotional commitment which cannot in the end be rationally justified. Those who urge the changing of current nuclear stances on moral grounds are thus often represented as well-meaning but irrational or anti-rational naïfs, out of touch or out of sympathy with the harsh realities of the modern world and borne along by their emotions to urge unreasoned and dangerous policies. Alternatively, attempts may be made to demonstrate the irrationality of the objectionable moral claims by philosophical argument. This variant of the defence of the *status quo* concedes that moral claims *can* to some extent be rationally supported, but denies that the claim that deterrence is immoral is proved.

That accusations of this kind should be made seem unsurprising when one surveys the literature. For there certainly is a style of *committed* moral argument, usually urging the immorality of current nuclear policy and the need therefore for radical changes of policy, which seems to make its case in a way visibly unlike the normal style of academic argument about morality; but it is arguments in the academic style which are usually assumed to be the prime candidate for rationality in this sphere. No wonder, then, that the committed style is suspected of irrationality, and that attempts are made to discredit its assertions. These attempts to discredit betray more anxiety than perhaps one might have expected. I suspect they are responses to, and hence an acknowledgment of, a persuasiveness the committed anti-nuclear style has which the austere calculations of the military strategists and administrators lack. Its appeal to morality gestures towards a dimension which the strategists leave out, but whose power to persuade they perhaps feel though they cannot correctly identify or approve it. I am interested in identifying and describing this persuasive extra element. Its detractors tend to stigmatize it as unrealistic idealism or emotional, subjective and excessive concern with morality, and to assume that such writing must be persuasive *not* because of its content, but because of its form – its literary qualities, its rhetoric, its aptitude to arouse emotion. But this seems too facile an analysis; I doubt if content can be so neatly divided from form. So I want to explore the possibility that the persuasiveness has as much to do with *what* is said as with *how* it is said. In that case it may be that to understand what is going on in these debates we need to rethink our view of what moral writing (writing about morality) *is*. That is what I attempt to do in this paper.

I have already suggested that there appear to be two distinct going styles of moral argument. (This volume contains examples of both.) The first task must be a more careful description of the two styles. For convenience I shall call proponents of an exhortatory or 'emotional' style *crusaders* and proponents of a philosophical or 'rational' style *casuists*. Crusaders and casuists do on occasion make use of each other's style; the label indicates which style predominates.

Crusaders want to change the world; they argue for the sake of making people do things. This style of moral writing typically attempts to awaken moral revulsion from some aspect of things as they are and to communicate both some vision of a better state of things and a belief in its possibility. It is the stuff of which reforming campaigns and revolutions are made; in both of these, political action is allied with and justified by changed and even seemingly paradoxical moral perceptions (property is theft; women are not angels but the slaves of men). This sort of moral argument is directed toward not the settlement of difficult, complex or borderline moral cases but at changed, or awakened, moral perceptions. It measures its success not by agreements reached over specific cases but by how widely its influence is diffused over a person's judgments and actions. This leaves a great deal of scope for disagreement over particular actions or policies among adherents of the same cause; what unites them is at least some central shared moral perceptions, some shared vision of the moral organization of the world, or of a fragment of the world. In CND, for instance, a core of shared ideas unites people more strongly than detailed differences of opinion divide them.

Since attacks on one's perceptions are threatening, moral onslaughts of this kind, if they do not produce enthusiasm, are liable instead to provoke angry and impatient rejection; for they seem to say things which obviously are not so (property is *not* theft – if there were no property, there could not be any theft;

119

women are not the slaves of men, since they freely accept their condition). It is, of course, possible for crusaders to counter these responses by producing resemblances between property and theft, or women and slaves; it is indeed normal for crusaders to back up their claims with argument, and if they are philosophers with casuistical argument, which has even been known to convince. (Or so many converts to religion claim.) Nevertheless crusading activities tend to make professional philosophers nervous. For crusading seems inimical to the detachment with which a professional intellectual ought to pursue truth. A crusader *cannot* be detached about the cause for which he is crusading, since he has already made up his mind about it. And since he wants to change the world, it is in his interest to awaken enthusiasm – faith being reputed to move mountains. But is there not something dangerous to reason, and to truth, in the awakening of enthusiasm? Does not the crusader use reason, if he does, in the service of enthusiasm? Should not intellectually respectable moral argument be of a quite different kind? And contemporary academic philosophy offers copious examples of this different kind: the moral arguments of the casuist.

The casuist, as the name suggests, typically argues difficult or disputed cases. The standard way to do this is by patient and often subtle analysis of paradigms and disputed cases whose object is to show that the disputed cases do or do not resemble some undisputed case sufficiently to be assigned the same moral standing. Thus in this volume Bernard Williams seeks to show that nuclear deterrence is objectively quite unlike accident control by tying babies to car bumpers. I shall be making considerable use of this example for purposes of illustration, so the reader may like here to refer to Williams's own account of the example, which will be found on p. 105 of this volume.

Do these descriptions suggest anything about the basis of the charge of emotionalism? In the case of nuclear policy, the object of anti-nuclear crusaders is to awaken us to the moral enormity of aspects of our nuclear stance which we may not have noticed or may prefer to forget, in the hope that perception of the enormity will induce us to work to change the policy. Casuistical rebuttals reject the blanket charge of enormity and try to show that though it attaches to some possible and perhaps to some actual pro-nuclear stances, it certainly does not attach to all. The object is presumably to neutralize the moral revulsion that crusaders might otherwise induce in relation to these arguably acceptable stances and thus remove a possible obstacle to their adoption. Now, if moral revulsion counts as an emotion – or even if it does not, but is normally or frequently associated with an emotion – then in a very obvious sense, crusaders in such debates appeal to emotion and casuists do not: for crusaders seek to arouse revulsion while casuists seek to get rid of it. But that they seek to arouse moral revulsion cannot in itself be an objection against the *moral* claims of the crusaders; and if in the process they *also* arouse emotion, this will merely be the result of the crusaders disagreeing with casuists in thinking a nuclear stance morally wrong, and of psychological facts about moral revulsion. In the context of moral argument, that crusaders try to arouse revulsion only justifies a charge of anti-rational emotionalism if supported by a theory of morality which says that moral judgment is essentially a matter for calm rational calculation which *any* influx of emotion is likely to distort, including the emotion often associated with moral revulsion; so that when seeking to show that moral revulsion is what is called for in some particular case, the philosopher should take special pains *not* to arouse emotion.

This, however, is only an unproven philosophical view, and moreover a highly controversial one. Certainly no philosopher has come up with an undisputed rational decision-procedure for settling doubtful cases in morality (other than the casuistical one); nor is there any reason to suppose that philosophers will or can. If the charge of irrational emotionalism in moral argument is to be more than expression of philosophical prejudice, it must reduce to the objection that the crusader does not use, or does not use properly, the only generally accepted method of moral argument – the rational methods of the casuist. In that case the claim would be that the crusader is irrational to the extent that he is not a casuist.

But to what extent is the crusader not a casuist? Does not he also at important points use exactly the casuistical method of comparison of the disputed case with a paradigm and the pointing out of similarities or differences? Property is *like* theft in that it deprives another of enjoyment of something to which he has a right; it is therefore bad for the same reason that makes theft bad. Wives are *like* slaves in that they suffer loss of autonomy, and labour for another without recompense or recognition of the real value of their labour. Or, using our illustrative example from this volume, nuclear deterrence is *like* putting babies on car bumpers. The crusader's method of argument is procedurally identical to the casuist's; the difference is in his striking examples, novel filing system (e.g. classifying property as theft, or wives as slaves) and his lack of interest in borderline cases. And *that* his filing should surprise is inevitable, given that he is trying to *change* moral perceptions. For his object is precisely to get us to see similarities which we did not see before. True, in order to make them visible he may have to supply a new context or perspective. But changing perspectives is the business he is in. It is not the business of the typical casuist, who uses the same method to file new cases along familiar lines.

Now, I would claim that it is a fact of human nature that changing perspectives runs a high risk of being an emotional business, both in that one whose perspective is changed is unlikely to remain entirely unmoved, and in that in order to produce a change in perspective it may be necessary to deliver an emotional jolt in the form of, say, a highly-charged example. (Like, for instance, babies on bumpers.) In other words, when attempts are being made to change perspectives, there is likely to be emotion around. This is another source of the charge of emotionalism. If a casuist interlocutor does not recognize or does not accept the revolutionary strand in the crusader's endeavour, then his (the crusader's) filing will seem quixotic and irrational and his use of highly-charged examples irresponsible and misleading. For of course a casuist staying within the old perspective will always be able to point out *dis*similarities between the cases the crusader is trying to assimilate (if they were not in some respects dissimilar, there would be no need for the crusader to try to assimilate them – and, from his point of view, no point in trying to either). In this situation a casuist will claim the crusader is saying things which are not true, and playing on the emotions of his readers to put over something which he could not put over by rational means. But the crusader cannot avoid giving the impression of wildness and irrationality, because the novelty of his filing system generates at least surface implausibility and possibly even paradox. He *may* perhaps avoid the appearance of emotionalism (by avoiding highly-charged examples). But then he may fail in his object (for instance his reader may not bother to look beyond his surface implausibility). So what can he do? Only protest that the casuist has missed the point.

Is it, however, *rational* to seek to change perspectives? That must depend on whether the situation calls for such a change. Paradoxes certainly *look* irrational; but crusading paradoxes are frequently devices for breaking down old perspectives. When is this appropriate? This is a large question to which I will return. Here I will only note that deterrence itself generates paradox – for instance, in the moral sphere, the paradoxes I sketched at the beginning of this paper; and in the practical, the paradox of making total disaster ever more possible and probable in order to prevent it happening. When paradox appears, something has to give somewhere. Rationality itself suggests that if we have arrived at this paradoxical solution, we must have got something badly wrong in the parameters of the problem, so that a change in perspective may not be quixotic but necessary for a rational solution. Even pro-nuclear casuists cannot avoid responding to this aspect of the problem, and in so doing becoming technically crusaders: for instance when they suggest it is not wrong to intend to do something wrong, they are in fact proposing a change in the existing moral filing system. What distinguishes them from overt anti-nuclear crusaders is not that one side avoids while the other embraces paradox (i.e. irrationality), but that the two sides differ over *what* has to give in order to avoid the nuclear paradox. How is one to decide which side has the better solution? Again this raises large questions to which I will return. But first I want to examine another attempt to substantiate the charge of emotionalism against crusaders.

It may now appear that in admitting that crusaders may need to deliver emotional jolts, I have conceded the main point against them. Could not casuists argue that whatever one's views on the philosophy of morals, nevertheless there surely is such a thing as morally and rationally reprehensible rabble-rousing – the provocation of one's audience to action by appeal to the non-rational elements in human nature, rather than to the rational elements? And is not the crusader delivering an emotional jolt doing exactly that? Take the example of babies on bumpers. An anti-crusading casuist might say: of course if we imagine babies really placed in this situation, it works powerfully on our emotions, and we recoil in horror. And that is exactly why the crusader chooses it: what else can be the *point* of such a bizarre example? But what should matter is not the violence of our recoil but exactly what it is about the example that makes us recoil at all. The crusader, however, is not interested in this. All he wants is to select some feature which the example shares with the disputed case, paying insufficient attention to whether it is indeed *that* feature from which we recoil, and thus by a kind of sleight of hand transferring the recoil from babies on bumpers to deterrence. But the transfer is illegitimate, for the two cases are simply not alike. In this particular example the feature selected is the placing of innocents in the firing-line: preventing accidents by putting babies on car-bumpers is wrong *because* it places innocents in the firing-line, and as deterrence does this too, we should recoil from it just as much as we do from babies on bumpers, according to the crusader. But, says the casuist, this is a case of illegitimate transfer. Thus, Williams suggests that the reason why we recoil from babies on bumpers is, roughly, that travelling around on bumpers is no life for a baby. It just so happens that in this particular case materially altering the babies' quality of life is *also* the placing of innocents in the firing-line. This is not so in the case of deterrence, which indeed places innocents in the firing-line but does not at all otherwise alter their quality of life. Our recoil, in the case of babies on bumpers, is our response to the sort of life babies are likely to lead on bumpers, *not* to their being, in that situation, innocents in the firing-line. Therefore it is a mistake to suppose that because we recoil from babies on bumpers, we ought to recoil from nuclear deterrence.

Certainly if what is said above of the crusader is true, he is guilty of mistaken analysis and misuse of the example. And it is certainly *possible* for him to do this out of excessive emotionalism: it is *possible* he made the mistake because he was too worked up, or that he misused the example because his motives were suspect. But his mistake could also just be a mistake, which had nothing to do with either his emotions or his motives. To find the source of a particular mistake one would have to look carefully at the particular crusader who made it. The casuist has not yet shown anything in crusading *procedure* as such which makes it more likely to produce mistakes than casuistry; he has simply offered a competing analysis of the example. Moreover, *has* he yet shown that the crusader really has made a mistake, and if so, how has he done it? He has shown that there is a difference between babies on bumpers and nuclear deterrence. But he has produced nothing to support his assumption that this difference is relevant to the disputed moral issue. And it is already perfectly obvious that accident prevention by babies on bumpers differs from nuclear deterrence in all sorts of ways. What needs to be shown is that the differences and similarities assumed to be relevant to the morality of deterrence really are so. (Williams himself does not explicitly make the relevance claim; though presumably he intends it, he certainly does not argue it.) If a casuist neglects to argue that the disregarded difference *is* morally relevant, he has no rational edge over a crusader assuming the opposite; both sides are simply making conflicting assumptions about moral relevance, and if this unsupported assertion of moral claims is supposed to indicate emotion and irrationality, each side is as emotional and irrational as the other. It is easy to miss this, because so much of the casuist's effort will have gone into detailing the differences, and we are so used to regarding the distinguishing of cases and analysis as rational philosphical procedure *par excellence*. But of course the crusader has done just the same sort of thing in finding a similarity. And *both* are in fact *looking to the moral intuitions of their audience* to support their relevance claim. In that respect they are both like, for instance, someone who tries to convince his audience that nuclear warfare is obscenely immoral by graphically describing its likely effects. All three offer their audience something as a candidate for test by moral recoil, in effect saying: in your heart do you believe it is morally right to do this? The opponent of nuclear weapons confronts them with the horrors of nuclear war. The crusader against deterrence in our example confronts them with a striking case of innocents in the firing-line. The pro-deterrence casuist might draw their attention to the misery of babies on bumpers.

If either the casuist or the crusader is to have the rational edge in this case (in the analysis of what is wrong about babies on bumpers), they must show not only that their own moral and relevance claims are supported by intuition, but also that their opponent's are not. But it seems to me that I recoil morally from babies on bumpers *both* because it is no life for a baby on a bumper *and* because it is putting innocents in the firing-line. Suppose, then, it is granted that both features are morally wrong and that nuclear deterrence is like babies on bumpers in that it is putting innocents in the firing-line, unlike it in that being in the nuclear firing-line leads to no accrual of misery. If putting innocents in the firing-line was a reason for moral objection to babies on bumpers, it is presumably still a reason for moral objection to nuclear deterrence, in the absence of arguments to the contrary. True, in the deterrence case we do not have the *additional* reason (accrual of misery) which is present in the case of babies on bumpers. But this does not show that there is *no* ground of moral objection or even that there is less ground for objection to deterrence than to babies on bumpers. (There may be all sorts of *other* grounds of moral objection peculiar to nuclear deterrence.) At this point it appears to be the crusader, *qua* opponent of deterrence rather than *qua* crusader, who must seem to have the rational edge, at any rate to those who share my moral intuitions about the example.

But now someone may want to say: 'Surely this means that the so-called rational method of moral argument, what has been described as the casuistical method, isn't really rational at all, since in the end it relies on intuition. Doesn't that make it just subjective and unreliable? What do you do if you get a conflict of intuitions? There doesn't seem to be any way the method could resolve that, so what use is it? Can't philosophers come up with something better than this?' The short answer to this is: 'No they can't. This is the best method of moral argument we've got, and we're stuck with it; so rather than throwing it away in disgust, I'd advocate understanding what it can and can't do. It can't resolve a conflict between unshakeable opposing intuitions; but strangely it can change some particular moral intuitions, when the method is used against a background of other, *shared* intuitions, and when the contenders both subscribe to rational values like consistency. This is its use, and it also means that though in a sense it *is* a subjective method, in that it presupposes some degree of subjectivity in moral judgment, it does not allow its users to be rampantly subjective: for its use implies membership of a moral community defined by shared intuitions.' In other words, the method relies on there being some degree of *agreement* in subjective moral judgments. However, not even a set of universally shared moral intuitions will get rid of all conflict, if these relate to general *kinds* of thing (as most widely shared intuitions seem to). For intuitions about general kinds may conflict with each other in particular cases, when these are simultaneously instances of different kinds (e.g. when joining the resistance is abandoning your family). The conflict may then be within the individual, and the casuistical method may be incapable of resolving it. In such a case all the individual can do is *choose*. It is the relevance problem again. This is not to say his action becomes totally arbitrary. There will still be reasons for the *action* chosen. But the reasons need not be compelling as reasons for the *choice* (hence the possibility of irresolvable conflict). This state of affairs is recognized by the importance we attach to the notion of moral autonomy. In a world with an objective, quasi-mechanical decision-procedure for settling moral questions, there would be no room for values such as freedom of conscience (not necessarily religious, but embodied in such things as, for instance, the right to conscientious objection to military service).

If this is how things are in relation to moral argument, however, crusading may now seem problematical. Can it in fact be in any way a rational activity? For if, as has been suggested, the crusader's primary purpose is to *change* moral perceptions, is he not in fact trying to disrupt the moral community? And if it is only *within* a moral community that moral argument can take place, must not moral argument be impossible for a crusader, who is operating from somewhere outside it? Does this not suggest that he is in fact *obliged* to use shock tactics, if he is to have any hope of success? And is not an obscure awareness of this the reason why charges of irrationality and emotionalism tend to be levelled against him? For if this is right then there *is* a structural reason for the shock tactics.

These questions call for some reconsideration of the description of crusading. First, is the crusader trying to disrupt the moral community? Well, he need not be trying to disrupt all of it, and when we consider what his 'shock tactics' consist in, he does not seem to be doing this. For the only 'shock tactic' yet mentioned is the use of examples which evoke a powerful moral and emotional response, i.e. the appeal to shared intuitions again. And to the extent that the crusader still shares intuitions, he remains *within* the moral community. But he can still try to change it piecemeal from within.

Consider from this point of view a crusader who thinks deterrence is morally objectionable, but does not think most people realize this. He will thus be trying to *change* the existing consensus of moral judgment. How he proceeds will depend on his diagnosis of why people currently judge wrongly, but one thing he will *not* be inclined to do is make a direct appeal to intuitions about deterrence: for the consensus being what it is, the appeal to intuition may go against him. This in itself puts pressure on him, as a member of a moral community, to think about why *he* thinks deterrence is immoral, i.e. he will look for that feature of deterrence which elicits his moral response. This will probably consist in trying to think of some other clearly immoral thing which deterrence is *like*: the casuistical method. Once he has found it, or thinks he has found it (it is possible for him to make a mistake), it will seem to him that the reason why others do not perceive the immorality of deterrence must be that they simply have not noticed this feature, or have not given it enough importance. It will seem, then, that the best thing for him to do to bring others round to his way of thinking is to point up this feature of deterrence in as dramatic and striking a way as possible, a way which gives it the salience he feels it deserves. For in deciding relative importance he may be exercising choice, i.e. going beyond argument. If others are to understand this choice they must see the world as he sees it. And to achieve this he may need to *light* deterrence in a particular way (hence 'seeing things in the same light'), a way which will throw into high relief that feature of deterrence in which he is interested (thereby inevitably obscuring other features which he regards as less relevant), and capture the attention of people who if left to themselves will not see anything here that particularly needs to be attended to. He may do this by, for example, likening deterrence to babies on bumpers. Hence his selective focus and use of powerful examples. These manoeuvres thus *are* dictated by the nature of the crusader's enterprise. But they are dictated *also* by the nature of moral argument, as we have it. I cannot see anything intrinsically reprehensible or irrational in these proceedings, though no doubt they can on occasion be reprehensibly and irrationally conducted. But that will be the fault of the individual crusader, not of crusading as such. Nevertheless to those who are not brought round to the crusader's way of thinking the proceedings are likely to appear both inept and reprehensible. But they should remember (as indeed should he) their own proceedings are going to appear just so to him. Their differences are going to appear irreconcilable as long as both sides fail to acknowledge that what is required for understanding the other position is an effort not just of rationality but also of imagination. To do them justice such arguments must be entered into before being fought. One may do one's best at this and still fail to see the world as the other sees it: it may still seem that deterrence just is not like, or not enough like, babies on bumpers. But it is idle to think that, given the current state of our understanding, this can be objectively proved. For 'like' here means 'like in all morally relevant respects'. And moral relevance cannot in the end be proved without recourse to intuition, gut feeling, or prior conviction, at any rate in the current state of the art.

Intuition, however, though it may be our last resort, may yet not take us all the way to our destination. Thus, everyone seems to share the intuition that nuclear war is a moral horror, but there is very little agreement over what follows from that – i.e. what are the implications for action of this judgment, and what *else* is a moral horror because nuclear war is (deterrence? flexible response? unilateralism? stasis?)? The casuistical method has been deployed on a grand scale to try to answer these questions, but with disappointing results. Let me now try to suggest why this might be, and to envisage some different way of proceeding.

II

So far I have been considering relatively marginal forms of crusading, involving not so much radical changes of moral perception as the activation and rearrangement of existing perceptions in which the casuistical method still plays a central role. But I think there may be changes of perception in which the casuistical method misleads more than it enlightens. It is possible for the conditions of life to change so drastically that the values with which one is already equipped are simply inadequate for dealing with the world. I am thinking of examples such as Colin

Turnbull's description of the Ik in his book *The Mountain People*. The Ik were a tribe for whom food became so scarce that the amount available could not support the existing numbers. What happened was that some individuals ate and others starved and died; those who ate ceased to have any concern for those who starved, regarding their misfortunes as matters for hilarity (as when an old woman fell down a ravine). What struck Turnbull was that the old woman laughed too: the weak seemed not to expect help but to acquiesce in their fate. When compassionate observers rushed to help, though, the weak sometimes broke down, and admitted remembering and longing for a time when things were different and people helped each other. Experiencing compassion again when, for very obvious reasons, it had disappeared from their world, made the present unbearable to them: they were no longer capable of the miracles of altruism which had hitherto sustained them.

One can view what was happening here as the emergence of a new morality suited to the exigencies of the time: the Ik could only bear the world as it was by thinking that (given the food situation) it was right that it should be as it was, that people should not help each other and that the weak should starve. Maybe what they did was literally make a virtue of necessity; which is one way of living with necessity. The new virtue was, however, initially incomprehensible to the compassionate observers who at first were taken up by their horror at the absence of the virtues (such as compassion) with which they were familiar. They found, though, that practice of those virtues did not *work* in this world: it simply made necessity harder to bear (for the observers could not supply enough food to feed all the people: they could not change the prevailing necessity). Their conviction of the universal validity of their own virtues, among *these* people and in *these* conditions, began to slacken: they began to find it possible to see the world as the Ik saw it, without a virtue of compassion. This was achieved not by crusading but by looking at the world of the Ik and imagining what it must be like to live in it.

Now, it is possible to look at the world and see accumulating changes in it whose *future* effects make new virtues necessary *now* (an analogue of the Ik's situation) without those virtues coming into being because the future effects are not certain or are not generally known or are too far off. Such a perception may give rise to radical crusading: the attempted creation of new virtues, which are what they are because of changes in the world, and are justified by these changes, not by making them out to be one of the old virtues in disguise. (Similarly old virtues can become obsolete. Thus most modern readers find some of the virtues listed by Aristotle in his *Nicomachean Ethics* incomprehensible *as virtues*.) I suspect that we are now in such a time of virtue-generating change, not just because of the existence of nuclear weapons but given the vast effect that individual human activity can now have, through technological advance, on the whole of the rest of the world. The individual action of relatively small numbers of people (those controlling governments and multinationals) can within the span of an ordinary life radically affect vast numbers of others and the natural world itself which supports us; nuclear war is only the most dramatic example of this. Another example is the diminishing of plant and animal species by land development and new methods of farming. Conversely, *large* numbers of people feel impotent to alter courses of action set by the few whose effects radically alter or threaten their own lives. All this, and nuclear weaponry in particular – not to mention other features of the modern world (such as its economic organization) – places us in the position of the Ik: plausibly, if we go on as we are we shall not survive.

This is a new situation and calls for new thoughts. We are confused about the implications of the immorality of nuclear war, confused about the morality of deterrence, because the immorality we *can* perceive is actually *new*. New crimes are now possible, as are new virtues. Of course these will bear *some* relation to familiar moral values; thus a possible new virtue such as concern for the preservation of species may be seen as related to the old virtue of thrift (which incidentally seems to have vanished from a world in which credit-card advertisers urge us to take the waiting out of wanting). And yet is is not *quite* like thrift, because (a) it is a virtue which institutions rather than individuals exercise, (b) more is involved in it than simply prudent provision for the future. Most conservationists would I think see more that is good in species conservation than just the biological prudence of keeping the gene-pool as large as possible; some seem to feel a sense that other species have a *right* to exist

Susan Khin Zaw

too; others that the richness and variety of the world is an intrinsic good. Because the new organizational structure of the world endows us with new capacities for good and evil, it demands new virtues of us, and in conjunction with our old viciousness, creates new vices. Because we do not clearly realize this we do not know how to handle the new moral situation even intellectually, let alone practically.

This may be granted, but now it may be said: why should the new thoughts which are called for be thoughts about *morality*? In the case of nuclear weapons at any rate, given the danger and the size of the mess, is not the first priority just getting *out* of the mess, i.e. averting the threat of universal destruction – never mind the morality of the mess itself or of features of it or of the means necessary to get out of it? Is not the most urgent problem one of *survival* – finding the most effective means of averting destruction – and not one of morality at all? The Ik, after all, adjusted their morality to the necessities of survival; but they settled on a means of survival first, the means being the crude biological one of the fittest surviving. Is not *that* the right parallel with our situation? Thus, suppose deterrence *is* the best means to survival. Then moral objections to it are irrelevant, just as compassion was irrelevant to the Ik's efforts to survive.

I would say to this: we have more time than the Ik (though perhaps not much). This creates problems. I cannot see the ditching of morality over nuclear matters as a workable solution, because, *having* more time, a lot has meanwhile to go on as before. The Ik could not tolerate the simultaneous existence of the old and the new virtues; the old compassion and the new altruism could not coexist. *We* cannot tolerate the simultaneous maintenance (for the purposes of ordinary life) and abandonment (for the purposes of nuclear policy) of moral values. Attempts might be made to justify this (the exclusion of morality from the nuclear sphere because survival is at stake) on familiar models, such as the justification of normally prohibited actions, e.g. deliberate killing of another person, in self-defence. But this seems to involve a view of morality as a system of prohibitions which lapse when survival is at stake – an unsatisfactory view on at least two counts: first, it suggests that the very same action can be wrong or not wrong depending on the circumstances. But killing in self-defence is held not to be wrong because it differs

132

internally (in its motivation) from murder; it is a different kind of action. Second, morality comprises not just the rejection of wrong things but the furtherance of right ones; to ignore this and view it as a system of prohibitions leads to impatience with morality at just the point where one would have expected it to have most to say – in the context of describing, not just what is *wrong* with the world, but how the world ought to be. Whether or not it is true, it is nevertheless *intelligible* that among the Ik the acceptance of death by the weak was experienced as a virtue (i.e. the way you ought to be if you were weak); and this should remind us that morality is not just a system of prohibitions for the restraint of anti-social impulses, but a *coherent* way of living in the world and enduring necessity.

This dimension is, I think, the extra element which informs the writing of crusaders and is conspicuously lacking from the calculations of military strategists and planners. Their projections of the future horrify us, not just because of the frightful suffering and killing anticipated, but because the future they anticipate, the suffering included, *makes no sense*. The deaths and suffering seem *pointless*. In a way it is unfair of us to be horrified; their brief does not include *making sense* of what may happen. They are supposed only to work out what to do if it does happen. But this is an absurd brief, for how can they determine, how could anyone determine, what should be done in a world which makes no sense? They can *obviously* only fulfil their brief within the framework of the way they make sense of the world as it now is. The paradox is, of course, that the state of affairs they anticipate is precisely the one in which so much havoc has been wreaked on the world as it now is that it *no longer has* the sense it has now. So when the decisions they make now become effective, the sense will have been removed from them.

The current British plans for civil defence against nuclear attack are a nice example of this: the plan seems to be to preserve a government structure by preserving the lives of key local government officers. In the state of affairs envisaged, this is the best that can be done to preserve Britain. But to preserve government structure will constitute preserving Britain only if there is enough left of what Britain is *now* after a nuclear attack for that structure to function recognizably as it does now. But this seems most unlikely. And if there is no functioning *social* structure, the 'government structure' will *then* be no such thing, but a selection of favoured individual survivors with means of force against other less favoured survivors. What sense is there in a government *now* taking care to bring about *that* state of affairs? Such a situation lacks human sense because it offends against justice, and it lacks even biological sense because it offends against function. There seems no reason why good local government officers should make good post-nuclear survivors or leaders. Thus those who urge that we exclude morality from our nuclear planning *now* seem to me to have become so hypnotized by the vision of this possible senseless future that they seek to bring forward some of its horrors to *now*, as if planning for a senseless future must itself be senseless. The senseless future infects the present and draws the present towards it. But to accept this is to forget that *that* future is only a *possible* future. Maybe the way not to make it actual is to try all the harder to envisage a possible future which *does* make sense and can be made actual, and aim for that. This is bound to seem unrealistic, for the world as it now really is seems to be headed for the senseless future. If so, then if we want to avoid it we must change the world.

Moralities, systems of values placed on actions and attitudes, are a central part of the enterprise of making sense of the world, and are thus part of what gives life meaning and hence survival its *point*. (Job despaired of the world when it no longer seemed to embody the moral order.) To urge those with functioning moralities to forget about morality in order to survive is thus like urging them, for the duration of the concern with survival, to concern themselves exclusively with survival while making survival itself pointless. (What is the point of surviving if *that* is what I have to do in order to survive?) This is surely the core of the controversy about the morality of deterrence. It seems to me undeniable that intending or threatening to fire off all the weapons *is not* as bad as it would be actually to fire them. But so what? That hardly justifies the policy or exhausts the moral unease it arouses. Now, the point of the debate about the morality or immorality of deterrence is usually seen as being this: if we decide it is immoral, we ought not to go in for it, whatever the consequences; but if we decide it is not immoral, it is all right to go in for it. But this question seems to fall short of the scale of the problem involved in deterrence, because it *ignores* the question of survival. I think the trouble is a false separation between morality and survival. The question we really want an answer to, the question which the nature of deterrence forces on us, is *not* the relatively restricted one about its morality (which as sometimes interpreted excludes questions about survival), but the wider and vaguer question about sense, to which morality is relevant but does not entirely determine: does deterrence make sense? *Does it* make sense to intend or threaten to do something terrible which makes no sense? What I claim for morality is that it is of its nature *relevant* to this question. But so is survival. Morality helps us to make sense of the present, but the present makes sense only if there is a (meaningful) future. If we have to exclude morality and sense from our contemplation of the future, or the possibility of the future from our morality, the present itself begins to lose *its* sense.

My suggestion, then, is that it is not useful to recommend the abandonment of morality with regard to nuclear policy in the interests of survival, because morality cannot be abandoned here without abandoning sense, and abandoning sense is not a possible way to live. We cannot simultaneously take and not take our morality seriously. Someone may now object: but people live like that all the time, by the simple device of selective blindness. Thus treatment of another that is not tolerated among the members of a particular group is regarded as wholly appropriate for those outside the group. The difference of treatment is not regarded as problematic because it is held, as a rule, to be justified by some actual difference between the two groups. This blinds those involved to any similarities there may also actually be which would tend to render the difference of treatment paradoxical. In answer to this, I would point out that the *need* for an aid to blindness shows that those involved feel themselves constrained by *rationality* – in the form of consistency in the application of their moral categories. Thus, in saying 'this is not a possible way to live', I mean not a possible way to live a *rational* life. One familiar form of crusading has been to seek to remove this selective blindness, and thus to bring under the protection of the moral community groups which had previously been excluded from it. Thus slavery and racism, for instance, have been attacked by insistence on justice and the brotherhood of man.

Crusading nuclear moralists are often attempting something similar. And in so far as their efforts are motivated by a desire for greater consistency in practical judgment, it is motivated by rational values (i.e. valuing the rational). This is why anti-nuclear crusaders often, in their turn, accuse their opponents of irrationality.

A similar thing applies to another arm of the attack on current policy. Defenders of deterrence on the whole do admit that even though it may be the best available option for avoiding war, nevertheless its own dynamic has brought and still brings a continual and increasing risk of war. They claim, however, that things being as they are, realism still requires us to recognize deterrence as the best hope, even though a world that has to rely on deterrence may be a doomed world. Such 'realism' does seem to require us to embrace a contradiction: for a chance of survival for the world which itself dooms the world is not a chance of survival. The more rational course would surely be to recognize that one of the assumptions which generate the contradiction must be false: either there is *no* very good chance of survival for the world, or deterrence is not that chance. This is a familiar enough crusading theme: since deterrence brings such great dangers, it is *not* realistic to treat it as the best chance of survival for the world, for the chance it offers is unacceptably small. It only appears to be the best chance because other (usually political) features of our world are regarded as fixed. Changing these may be difficult, but one of the things that makes it difficult is our belief that we cannot change them. Since deterrence offers such a poor chance of survival, changing these supposedly immutable features of the world *must* offer a better chance – and so, to improve our chances, we *must* believe we can. It is rather like Pascal's bet on the existence of God: if we lose the bet, we only lose something we never had. But if we win, we win everything. So *it is rational* to bet – on God, or on our ability to change things. Thus the attack on current policy can again be seen as a demand for *greater* rationality in practical matters, not less.

Obviously to gamble rationally one must assess the probabilities as accurately as possible; but in this case (though of course one must take account of as many relevant *facts* as one can) still assessing the probabilities is inescapably a matter of judgment.

For judging what can be changed depends on judging probabilities of human behaviour, and there is no science of that sufficiently detailed and established to yield the sort of reliable predictions which would make assessment of probabilities a matter of calculation rather than judgment.

I want now to deal with another possible objection to the very idea of changed moral perceptions. I have been suggesting that the pressure for a new morality can come from the necessities of survival. But, it may be said, this begs the crucial question of the relation between morality and prudence (survival being the most urgent task of prudence). The so-called 'necessities' of survival are necessities only if survival itself is regarded as a necessity. But it is not, and morality has never regarded it as such. Take the Ik. Maybe they did as a group effectively, even if not consciously, choose that the fittest of them should survive, and adjust their morality to suit. But they did not have to choose that. They *could* have chosen to maintain their old system of values governing human relationships and accept the collective death which would have been the price of it. Would not this, in fact, have been the *truly* moral alternative, as acknowledging the supremacy of moral over prudential values? It is, after all, possible for us to prefer death to dishonour, and we regard those who do as morally admirable. In deciding what we think of the Ik we should compare them to, say, someone living under a corrupt régime which makes right living inconsistent with survival. We consider the morally right (though difficult) course for such a person to be to continue to live rightly and accept the death which will be the consequence, rather than to betray his values in order to survive. Just so the Ik should have accepted death rather than betray their original values. Otherwise we end up with the conclusion that whatever is, is right – the antithesis of all morality. For an individual in some régimes is just as impotent, the conditions of life laid by the régime are just as much a necessity for him/her, as the conditions of life laid down for the Ik by their position in the natural and political world. It is sophistry to distinguish between the abandonment of morality and the change of moral values when confronted with the issue of survival in the nuclear age. Our situation may indeed be that, like the Ik, we have to *choose* between morality and survival.

I accept that the relation between morality and survival is

crucial here, but I think the analogy with the Ik fails at this very point. For *whose* survival is at stake? In the case of the Ik, normal values seem to have been abandoned for the sake of the survival of some individuals, either *qua* individuals or *qua* members of the tribe, by whom the tribe could perhaps be regenerated in some possibly better future time. The parallel case to this in the case of nuclear war seems to be that of the individual nation: discussing nuclear policy and deterrence purely from the point of view of whether *Britain*, say, or at least some of the people in it, was going to survive. Now, individual Britons might well feel an overriding concern with this which was essentially prudential in origin. The survival at stake for a Briton thinking in these terms is in a sense always *my* survival – either *my own individual* survival or the survival of *my people*. Similarly with the Ik. It is not, however, in these contexts conceived as a moral necessity *that I or my people should survive*. On the other hand, it is when we try to think about the problem as a whole and not from an individual or national point of view that the imperative of survival in the context of nuclear war seems most compelling. I suggest that this is precisely because the question of survival is then *not* considered from an individual point of view and is therefore felt at least partly as a *moral* rather than a prudential imperative. For those threatened by an all-out nuclear war are not particular people or classes or nations, but an indefinitely large proportion of the whole of humanity (not to mention an indefinitely large slice of non-human nature which currently sustains it). Nuclear threat forms a *de facto* collective whose membership is unknowable and which is represented by no existing political or cultural or social group with which one might now as an individual feel identified. The collective is bonded together by nothing more than their common humanity (and if we include threatened nature, not even that) and their common danger. This gives a new, dark meaning to the idea of the brotherhood of man and the human (or natural) community: we are now indeed all members of one another, because very many of us are threatened by the same man-made death, and any one of us – impossible to tell which – may belong to that many. It is the survival of the collective that we feel it imperative to ensure, and *not* just because each of us may be a member of it (or otherwise why not just dig our own fully-equipped hole in the ground?). That at least must be what is implied by the generally accepted view that nuclear war is a moral horror. It is so because in waging nuclear war, far from ensuring survival of the collective, we kill it off; we fail in a *moral* duty to something other than and more important than ourselves. *This* imperative of survival is thus a *moral* imperative. And I think it is also a *new* moral imperative, because it enjoins concern for a new entity, for something other than individuals or existing social entities. The old duties of compassion and benevolence no doubt enjoin concern for the fate of the members of the collective as *individuals*, but I do not think nuclear war seems unquestionably a moral horror just because it will cause a very large number of individuals to perish horribly. For much more than that will be destroyed; not just the individuals but most of the structures which support them and the achievements which have given their life meaning. The crime is not just killing people but causing chaos to come again, or rather *creating* chaos out of order. If this were actually to happen I cannot believe it is not part of human nature to see it as other than a transition from a better to a worse state, not just for a particular person undergoing it but *in itself*. (I should add that I regard aversion to pain as likewise part of human nature, despite the existence of both masochists and neurological variation. 'Human nature', as I use it, is a normative concept.) If moving from order to chaos is thus a human disaster, then failure to prevent it is a moral failure – indeed the failure of morality itself. Similarly, I think we feel a moral requirement to prevent the destruction of the collective over and above the requirement to concern ourselves with the fate of its members as individuals. We thus feel a moral requirement of concern for a *new entity*, which I would therefore call a new moral requirement.

I have no designation for this entity other than vague expressions like 'humanity as we know it'; or perhaps the new concern is for the collective plus what sustains it, in which case the entity might be 'human society and nature as we know it'. (Finding a better designation than this is a task for moral philosophy.) The entity has in a sense been created by the fact that there is now a way to express *lack* of concern for it: nuclear war. Military technology has made this entity thinkable in concrete terms, and we have tried to rise *morally* to the occasion by confusedly seeing destruction of the new entity as a crime, and overriding concern for its survival as a duty. In this respect, concern for survival in the case of nuclear war is different from the concern for survival of the Ik, who were concerned with their own survival in a very familiar sense. The cases become more like each other if we think of the new, nuclear-threatened collective as a tribe to which we *all* belong; but this seems a purely intellectual manoeuvre in the absence of anything binding the members of the collective together at all analogous to the sorts of things which bind the members of a tribe together in such a way as to *make* them all members of one tribe. That is precisely the problem: there is no tribe to look after the members of this collective. Another way of seeing the efforts of the crusaders is as the start of an attempt to *create* such a sustaining tribe, by at least getting the members of the collective to think of themselves as a tribe, and thus have some hope of creating the social and political structures necessary to bring the tribe concretely into being and protect its interests. It will, however, be a tribe quite unlike any others, if only in that ideally it includes *everybody*.

I have been suggesting that the imperative of averting nuclear holocaust is a moral as much as a prudential imperative. Someone may now say: 'Of course it is a moral imperative, and what your argument shows is that it is moral precisely because it *isn't* prudential. That is what is wrong with your interpretation of the Ik: their abandonment of compassion was immoral precisely because it *was* prudential. You still haven't answered the claim that the Ik *ought* to have chosen death rather than callousness. What about the analogy suggested between the case of the Ik and that of the individual living under a corrupt régime?'

I think there is a difference between the choices facing the Ik and the choices facing such an individual which affects their moral perceptions and hence what can be said to be morally required of them. It is a question of how their choice appears to them, of what it is they seem to themselves to be choosing. We regard the heroic dissident's choice of death as obviously right because we see his acts and choice as taking place within the context of ongoing societies (his and our own) for which his choice is *significant*. His choice of death is a comment on the régime. Since societies continue even though the individual does not, his death seems worthwhile both to us and to him because there is always the possibility, perhaps the hope, that *someone* will see its significance, will read correctly what it says (even if it is only his killers). Belief in its significance is what makes it worth doing. One may think here of Auden's poem 'In Memory of W.B. Yeats':

Time that is intolerant
Of the brave and innocent . . .

Worships language and forgives
Everyone by whom it lives.

This might suggest that we value such acts because though men die, the word lives. It is true that words, and significant acts, last longer than those who make them; but even the word lives only as long as it is heard. Signifiers must signify *to someone*. Suppose now that the Ik do choose collective death rather than the abandonment of compassion: when they have died their death for the sake of virtue as they conceive it, for whom will this supreme sacrifice be *significant*? Awareness of a significance-conferring context makes the heroic dissident's sacrifice seem good by allowing him to see it as having a point beyond his own personal concerns, and hence a point he can die for: for though he loses *his* future, there is still a future – the future of the context which gives his death significance. The difference with the Ik is that they stand to lose, not just a personal future, but *the* future: in their situation, choosing compassion means choosing the death not just of individuals but of the tribe. The act itself destroys the context which gives it significance, and thus in its accomplishment becomes merely a meaningless suicide. Perhaps the significance-conferring context need not be human: religion may supply a view of the world as a society or ordered set of beings of which human society is only a part. If the Ik have such a religion it is conceivable that collective death could appear to them, in the context of the world supplied by religion, as morally required. But *without* a context, I do not think such a collective death can appear as other than pointless suicide. And I do not think morality can require such a suicide: *that* is the link, in such cases, between morality and survival.

If the above fails to convince, consider the following case.

Suppose that in the nuclear aftermath two small social groups are the last people left on earth. The groups are normally in contact with each other. Leaving a religious justification aside, what would be the morally right thing to do in the following circumstances: one group falls sick of a contagious disease and becomes helpless. All will die without help. There is a good chance that some will survive if helped, but a near certainty that the other group will catch the disease too and also die if they approach and help the sick ones. If they help, there is a near certainty that human life on earth will cease; if they do not, there is a chance that it will continue. Without a religious or other-worldly justification, who will say that the right thing for them to do is obviously to help the sick? Can not we imagine the sick accepting their death and not asking for or expecting help, so that humanity might live? Would that not be virtue, and the forgoing of compassion by the other group, wisdom? Would maintenance of compassion, in these circumstances, not be senseless suicide? And would that not seem just not to be an option, as in normal circumstances suicide is regarded as not an option? There is a reason why suicide has seemed both irrational and a crime, and I think the reason is that there is a self-evidence in the assertion that something is better than nothing. Survival of some thus just is better than survival of none, and so it is a moral requirement to ensure it (our duty is to prefer the good). For by that survival even those that do not survive retain awareness of a possible future in which their death has significance, and so moral worth. There is perhaps another lesson to be drawn from this. Maybe governments should now remember not just their duty to those they govern, but also their duty to the threatened nuclear collective. Maybe on occasion the interests of this override the interests of the governed, and make national suicide obligatory if the alternative really is *total* loss of the future (i.e. loss of *everyone's* future). Maybe this is a closer analogy to the man under the corrupt régime.

To conclude with a summary: some crusading is an imperfectly understood struggle to create the new values we need not only to survive but to live endurably in the world we have made, that is, to continue to find meaning in our lives in it. Because we have more time than the Ik there is time for rival moral creations to emerge (typically in the form of proposed political solutions: but political solutions always carry strong moral implications within them). How are we to assess them? I cannot offer anything more helpful than this: *not* by harking back always to old models, but by measuring them against the world (are things like this? Is this what is needed to ensure survival?) and against ourselves (is this liveable? Does it speak to our condition?). If the answer to all these questions is 'yes', then what is proposed *must be* (however impossible current circumstances may make it look). That is the true, and rational, imperative of survival.

The Great Wall of China. Notes on the Ideology of Nuclear Deterrence

Rip Bulkeley

> Far rather do I believe that the high command has existed
> from all eternity, and the decision to build the wall likewise.
> Unwitting peoples of the north, who imagined they were the
> cause of it! Honest unwitting Emperor, who imagined he
> decreed it! We builders of the wall know that it was not so,
> and hold our peace.
>
> from Franz Kafka's *The Great Wall Of China*

I

The traditional case against nuclear weapons rests on several
interrelated grounds. They are morally unjustifiable, extremely
dangerous in several separate and cumulative ways, politically
hampering, militarily useless, and economically destructive of the
societies that wield them and all others. I shall for the sake of
brevity refer to this powerful critique as the liberal case against
nuclear weapons and doctrines, thereby promoting a single
distinguishing epithet to represent a cluster of related ones, such
as 'middle-class', 'petty bourgeois', 'utilitarian', 'empiricist', and
others, which may be understood with occasional exceptions to
be connoted by it. By this I mean to imply at least the following.
The traditional indictment of nuclear weapons is made out with
reference to real aspects of them, and ones which are really
objectionable, giving sufficient grounds for desiring their abol-
ition in general and their renunciation by Britain in particular.
What the liberal case lacks, however, is a grasp of what nuclear
weapons really are, which is to say, what social relations they

embody, maintain and fulfil. While an understanding of these realities may not be needed in order to protest against the existence and call for the renunciation of nuclear weapons, it is arguable that it is required if we are ever actually to get rid of them. Without such understanding, the past twenty-five years of inconclusive liberal objections could well be extended to fifty, unless the increasingly likely holocaust supervenes.

Things are seldom only what they appear to be. So stirs the hunch of reason in every human epoch, and Marx's frequent remarks to the same effect were little more than the truisms of a received tradition, spiced with a version of Hegel's 'ruse of reason' device. But in treating the doctrines of nuclear deterrence as ideological, I expect to place myself straightforwardly in debt to Marx's reworking of the Hegelian philosophy. For readers unfamiliar with that reworking and the intellectual schools which have flourished in its aftermath, a short and necessarily abstract sketch of the marxist notion of ideology follows, together with a list of issues which it throws up in respect of nuclear deterrence.[1] Later sections begin the discussion of the issues in more detail.

By ideology, then, I understand a structured discourse through which people in a class-divided and hence internally alienated society apprehend the reality of their world, and through which also they intend and organize their actions. Such a discourse is labelled 'ideology' to draw attention to its deficiencies both as to truth and as to efficacy in serving human needs, deficiencies which can only be perceived in part from within the society itself.[2] Within our own class-divided society of late and increasingly state capitalism, most ideological confusions still have to do with the substitution of terms denoting real or fictional things (often, commodities) for terms referring directly to relations between people.[3] This phenomenon in the history of ideas is known as 'reification', and is one of the principal ways in which people see their own society as other than in fact it is, thereby frustrating many of their basic needs as human beings.

These misperceptions by a majority, however, may serve the turn of a privileged and powerful minority, in whose distorted interests the entire social order functions. But though this is true, it needs careful qualification. Ideological appearances, though deceptive in one sense, are no mere mirages. Precisely because they structure people's interactions in the world, they enter into

daily human reality as a mass of interlocking practices, arrangements, customs and institutions. Wages, marriage, and the jury
system are all examples of the unity of social reality with
ideological appearances, necessary to the functioning of any
class-society, which I shall claim is also present in the case of
nuclear deterrence. It is this which gives ideology its peculiar
character of being both true and false, so to speak, both fact and
illusion. And which in turn can lead to endless confusion in the
social struggle to abolish or even merely to reform such practices.

For it is a mistake to think that ideology is the deliberate result
of some conscious conspiracy of those who benefit, relatively,
from its effects. Nor is it simply a matter of the unconscious self-
deceit of those who take part, whether as losers or as gainers, in
ideological discourse, as if they could be freed from it merely by
some simple, verbal and rational therapy. What we actually are
as human beings, in the contingent context of our present class-
society, is constituted by relationships with others which could
not obtain, unless sustained by and sustaining those radically
defective accounts of what is going on which are our ideology. In
short, how people live, what they are, and how they see
themselves as living are not separate aspects of the human world.
If any of them is to change, they must all do so.

For nuclear deterrence to be revealed as ideology, therefore, I
shall need at the very least to suggest convincingly that its
illusions arise from aspects of social reality. To do this will be to
ask why our society has to appear to be what it is not, for most
people most of the time, in order to remain what it actually is, in
the particular sphere of nuclear weapons deployment. Do nuclear
weapons have functions which could not be achieved if they were
widely recognized? And why are just those stories told about
nuclear weapons which are told, rather than others? Are the
typical inversions of capitalist ideology, familiar to marxists in
other fields, present also in this one? Is the nuclear arms race
sustained by thinking which abstracts the facts from their social
contexts, with a deceptive empiricism which misinterprets rather
than falsifies them? Does the dogma of nuclear deterrence rely
on superficial concepts, applied with ahistorical sloppiness, to
achieve its mystifications? And do they in turn lead those
oppressed by nuclear weapons into pessimism and powerless
negativity, thereby preventing the development of social alterna-

tives to the nuclear labyrinth? It depends on the answers to these questions, whether nuclear deterrence is a case of ideology in the marxist sense.

Before discussing them further, I shall mention the difficulty I experience in trying to do so. There is no marxist study of ideology in the sphere of military strategy known to me. Marxist groups engaged in the campaign against nuclear weapons seldom go beyond what I called above the liberal case, fortified by calls for agitation amongst and action by the working class. On the other hand many observations I shall make can be met with, if expressed in rather different terms, somewhere in the more radical and socially conscious part of the spectrum of liberal anti-nuclear literature. Perhaps my only contribution will be to see those points as relevant to different questions than the usual ones.[4]

II

One seeks in vain in the classical marxist critiques of capitalism or their modern sequels for chapters headed 'Force' alongside the magisterial accounts of 'Money', 'Wages', 'Surplus Value' and so on. It is as though the opponents of capitalism had conspired with their enemies to pretend that the sphere of purely economic factors, which it was their business to expose as a fraud, really existed after all. But there is one group of marxist writings, now over sixty years old, which offers a starting point from which to approach our topic. They are the works of Bukharin, Liebknecht and Lenin on the related questions of imperialism and militarism.

Besides other forecasts which have received little confirmation to date, such as that small states would soon vanish from the world system, these writers correctly pointed out the necessity for the military functions of states growing vastly in importance, as the planet became completely allocated into territorial states and between rival imperialisms. As the finite imperialist solution to the problems of leading capitalist ruling classes became less and less effective, so each state would need to spend more cash and political effort on its military functions. Amongst other effects, this would support the costly new version of imperialism, under which additional assets had now to be seized from a rival

Rip Bulkeley

capitalist empire rather than from pre-capitalist societies. It could
also act as a direct subsidy to key firms, and prime the home
market with the wages of soldiers and of workers in large-scale
weapons, or waste, production. The history of our century can
therefore be seen as the following contradiction. On the one
hand there is the traditional need of capital to compete with its
rivals by growth and amalgamation, which by our day has come
to require the negation of state frontiers, to the point where even
the boundary between the rival imperialisms of East and West is
undergoing significant erosion. On the other, capital has an
increasingly desperate need to use force both within and between
nations, and thus for states which are strong both militarily and
as units of capital.[5]

One of my main themes in what follows will be the suggestion
that nuclear and other mass weapons and their related doctrines
have an importantly unstraightforward part to play on the second
side of this contradiction, the one concerned with coercion and
discipline. The ever more dominant state sectors of capital are
not best suited or best served by appearing to those whom they
exploit with the frankness of the employer-employee relationship
of the private sector. Even in societies where state capital
controls the lion's share of the economy, most workers are hired,
fired, paid and controlled by the enterprise or firm. Those who
make up the state are far from anxious to reveal themselves as
the common employers of all, or most, or a large minority of
people, for fear of obvious questions as to why all participants in
this nominally collectivist social arrangement may not share
equally in the goods produced. And yet the state as one of the
chief bearers of capital in any modern society is directly
interested in, and responsible to the rest of the ruling class for,
the discipline and control of labour. Though deepening crisis
makes this more and more difficult, state capital often prefers
more indirect methods to the direct negotiated coercion by which
private capital still squares up to labour. The state treats labour,
for preference, less as workers than as citizens, less as the bearers
of special skills, more as an undifferentiated mass. Across-the-
board wages policies are one reflection of this.

Another less obvious one is that surveillance, intimidation and
indoctrination now tend to be applied in a general indiscriminate
fashion. In such a climate, a state's possession of mass terrorist

148

weapons,[6] where it can acquire them, seems highly appropriate. It is an irrelevance that in every nuclear weapons state the pointed end of such weapons is directed towards some enemy society. All such threats of annihilation are mutual and therefore reflexive. An instinctive appreciation of this sustained the initial wave of horror and alarm which swept the USA immediately after its rulers had first developed and used nuclear weapons, and long before any enemy was expected to acquire them. The reflexiveness of nuclear threat is nicely illustrated by the willingness of many governments to build nuclear weapons even for potential enemies with only conventional means of attack, in the form of power stations already 'delivered' to the home territory. In general, nuclear weapons have the vital function of the threat of last resort between any ruling class and its own working class. As illustrated by recent events in Poland, nuclear terrorism can be used to set the permissible limits to political change within either of the two great empires. It has perhaps replaced fascism as the preferred form of barbarism for desperate rulers, if ever the only other option came to be socialism. And all this of course now depends on mutual possession of mass weapons and on a system of opposition between rival power blocs.

But nuclear weapons are attuned to the other side of the central contradiction also. As the largest independent units of capital become more and more globally agglomerated, so it becomes both more difficult and more crucial to obstruct or at least delay any parallel development on the side of labour, a process made superficially more probable by the new communications and information technology. Here too nuclear weapons can serve their owners well. The absolutely destructive character of the weapons deployed by the necessary enemy transfers itself to become, first, the idea that the enemy is absolutely evil (thus, of course, an appropriate target for 'our own' weapons), and second, the myth that this absolute negative Other is a rival empire in every way separated from 'us'. Where the second idea is repeatedly contradicted by facts of global interdependence, so that these cannot be easily suppressed, they become the objects of a special political exasperation which is all their own.[7]

This way of seeing nuclear weapons can improve our understanding of the arms race. Neither the doctrine of nuclear deterrence, nor liberal charges of 'over-kill' and 'first-strike', do much to explain just why such vast and militarily superfluous arsenals have in fact been acquired by the superpowers.[8] But if two important functions of the nuclear armoury are the amount of general intimidation it produces in the working class of the home empire, and the degree of effective mistrust it helps to sustain between working classes in rival empires, it seems probable that there is a factor of habituation which must needs be perpetually overcome by weapons innovation, so as to raise terror and suspicion once more to the required pitch.[9] Interestingly, there is no such thing as 'over-terror' in the system.

There are of course other straightforwardly functional aspects to nuclear weapons, such as their role in transferring values from labour to capital via non-competitive state contracts, their alleviation of under-consumption problems through large-scale expenditure on waste, financed through the state by taxes on capital in commodity-producing industries, and their diversion of potentially competing capital out of the world market. Such broadly Keynesian functions have been little affected by the advent of versions of monetarism to political power in two nuclear states. But since they are already discussed in the literature, and since I do not believe them to be so closely related to the ideological discourse of nuclear deterrence as the other functions mentioned above, I shall proceed to examine those in more detail.

III

Having already touched on one example of it, I shall begin a more detailed survey of ideological aspects of nuclear deterrence by looking at instances of the phenomenon known as inversion. That is what one finds when conventional truisms turn reality back to front, as when, for example, it is claimed that firms are run for the benefit of their employees, or that in Britain the people have power over the state. The example already touched on had to do with where nuclear weapons were aimed, and who or what was being deterred. Overt doctrine on both sides of the Iron Curtain is that the rulers of Side A only deploy these regrettably genocidal objects so as to deter the rulers of Side B from ever using theirs. But concealed within the avowed nuclear terrorism of superpower rulers towards each other's society is another unavowed but possibly more important terrorism, directed against their own working class in each case, and also against the development of any unity amongst working people around the world. Far from defending its own people and deterring the enemy state, Side A's nuclear deterrence is about deterring their own labour force and, by providing the necessary external threat, about defending the supposedly enemy rulers against their own people.

Other inversions are related to this one. So-called provision of security is in fact its reckless squandering. So-called civil defence is mainly about defending the state against its own civil society, and partly also, in the West, about the privatization of protection through a domestic shelter industry.[10] Chomsky has suggested that deterrence works so as to present states which are objectively opposed to each other as if they were allies, and vice versa.[11] His claim is more convincing, in my view, if it is applied to classes. Also relevant here is the view of Günther Anders,[12] that nuclear weapons, though apparently dividing the world between opposing terrors, have in fact united it through a negative universality, namely their capacity as the increasingly probable liquidators of planetary civilization. It is not just that the clearest evidence that human beings now live in a single society, even if we do not yet live in it *as* one, is our ability to destroy it in a single complex historical event called the Third World War. It is also that this negative universality has to be achieved through and for the thwarting of any true and positive universality in human relationships. The reason being that neither the Western nor the Eastern versions of capitalism could possibly survive the constructive internationalization of human society.[13]

A more general feature of ideology than inversion is alienation, above all in the form of reification. If people's real needs are to be largely frustrated, and their productive capacities stunted, distorted and made over for the benefit of a minority of armed exploiters, as is everywhere more or less the case, then it is neither bearable for them nor safe for their oppressors that this should be clearly and frankly and constantly recognized by all parties. In modern societies organized around the processes of commodity exchange, concealment and distortion of people's real relationships are often achieved by projecting them on to various real or fictitious non-human entities. By this means contingent, historical facts come to be seen as absolute, universal or natural ones, which cannot be altered no matter how unpleasant.

Nowhere is this ideological transmutation more striking than in people's ideas about the arms race, be they its accusers or excusers. The phrase 'arms race' itself, which summarizes the myth that relations between the superpowers are centrally concerned with the technical details of the acquisition of arrays of lethal but dumb engines, is a good place to start. And I have already mentioned the way in which a supposed enemy, and the reason for their being an enemy, are assimilated to the weapons they may or do possess. Then there is the common attitude, fostered by politicians claiming that 'nuclear weapons can't be disinvented',[14] which takes nuclear weapons to be somehow themselves the cause of the arms race, being almighty, indestructible, irresistible, perpetually self-developing, and unswervingly dedicated to the destruction of humanity.[15] But the political, historical power ascribed to nuclear weapons is really our own power cast into a false and negative form and alienated from us. It is the opportunity and ability of human beings in this epoch as in none before to organize ourselves as a world society. We let that power be alienated from us in fact and in ideology at our peril.[16]

An important aspect of reification in nuclear deterrence has been a tendency for both sides of the debate to think of security as a matter of weapons, as many ordinary voters do, whether of their deployment or their renunciation. In a later section I shall mention the effects of this on movements for nuclear disarmament. Here I want to look at its influence in pro-deterrence quarters.

The protection of society is not merely alienated from its citizens, more than ever before, by the utopian[17] single-weapon doctrine which sees nuclear weapons as the essential guarantee of world peace. It is also being alienated from the military themselves. Instead of holding nuclear weapons as the instruments of their own intentions, they find themselves cast as servants and appendages of weapons, in whose structure and selection both strategic and sometimes even tactical decisions confront them as already taken. It is not, as Anders suggested, that the weapons have seized the capacity for action from their nominal wielders. It is just that the proportion of past and unalterable decisions to open future ones has become unbalanced.[18] Increases in automation appear to those who handle nuclear weapons as though they were breaking free and taking over. At the same time, due to the impossibility of using them in combat for any finite, rational ends, the military have lost their former believable organic relationship with the rest of society. It has been replaced with one that is more formal and abstract, sustained not by tradition and practice, but only by the theoretical constructs of hypothetical reason. It is as though the medical profession, faults and all, were suddenly to find itself deprived of the entire pharmacopoeia, at least for serious cases, and left with nothing but euthanasia pills to give people in extreme pain. There might grow up a medical ideology of 'terminal deterrence', claiming boundless beneficial effects on patients from the knowledge that such pills might be given them if they were to get too ill.

As for reification in vulgar political applications of nuclear deterrence doctrine, examples are two a penny in every gutter from Fleet Street to Whitehall. In the present debate over NATO's famous new land-based intermediate range missiles, for instance, all that is allowed to matter in some published contributions is Soviet deployment of such-and-such missiles. Discussion of the context in which the relevant Soviet decisions were taken early in the 1970s, or of current Soviet political intentions, is as irrelevant to the interests as it seems to be beyond the competence of many of the powerful opinion-formers and decision-takers involved. But when there is so much disregard for factors which should be relevant, were the pretended functions of nuclear weapons the real ones, the probability of their having other functions such as those suggested here is enhanced. And if these other functions are at all as I have suggested, they could only be achieved in a society which operates under the collaborative reticence and confused distractions of ideology.

The emperors of East and West, with their tax-fed henchmen, need to believe that the great nuclear wall has been their own rational decision, and that its sole benevolent purpose is to keep out the hordes of the barbarian enemy. They need to believe this themselves and have it believed by others so as to give the necessary orders and preach the necessary doctrines with conviction. All the same, the key to understanding the nuclear wall is to grasp its function in warding off other threats, threats which may not be spoken of for fear that naming them would bring closer the day of their realization, which is to say, a day of the end of empires.

IV

In this section I shall look more closely at the complex relationships between the ideological surface of nuclear deterrence and its covert, inadmissible, but essential social reality. I shall do this by listing some of the evasions, confusions and contradictions of deterrence, whose presence is to be expected on my hypothesis. In two groups of cases I shall suggest ways in which the deceptive appearance arises from the reality it conceals.

I have heard it suggested that inconsistencies and contradictions are stronger evidence for the ideological nature of any account of the world than are falsehoods, evasions, or the misleading selection of facts. The latter are harder for a critic of ideology to establish, for both practical and theoretical reasons, than the former. And beside those advocates of nuclear deterrence who build their case with the aid of such cheap tricks, others can probably be found, more honest, intelligent and scholarly, who do not. That some writers argue for deterrence in a corrupt fashion does not show it to be a corrupt theory. (Though if the proportion of such formulations on the pro-deterrence side were very high, something not at all easy to prove of course, it might be suggestive of a link of some kind, on 'like draws to like' lines.) But in any case there is a close link between truth and consistency. Where the latter is so frequently thrown to the winds, there too must truth have been often disregarded.

One of the boldest distortions in the Western version of deterrence doctrine is the claim that NATO deploys nuclear weapons to counter those of the Soviet Union. So much history is set aside by this tale, such as which states first made, used and began stockpiling atomic bombs, and which first formed a military alliance centred on a nuclear strategy, that one is tempted to regard it as a ritual incantation without even a pretence to truth. Contempt for facts is a commonplace in the explanations of their nuclear weapons put out by both super-powers, as for example when they focus on particular weapons developments and remain silent on others, so as to be able to denounce the other side as provocative leaders in the arms race. Another common device is simple vagueness. Thus it is rare to hear an advocate of deterrence define what is to count as aggression, rarer still to hear one given which is neutral between the interests of both blocs. One very important use of vagueness concerns just what nuclear weapons are supposed to deter, whether use of nuclear weapons by the enemy, use of conventional weapons in major war, enemy support for proxy wars in the underdeveloped borderlands, enemy political or economic gains within 'our' sphere of interest, or what.

Direct omission of facts is so common in the state information and opinion-moulding system that one hesitates to suggest there is any special reason for it in the case of nuclear deterrence. Ministry of Defence hand-outs on the Euro-strategic missile balance, which fail to mention NATO's Tornado programme or the US Poseidon fleet at Holy Loch, are so normal in our democracy that it is small wonder no one even blushes when exclaiming in disgust at the official philosophy of the Soviet Union, which actually endorses lying and the breaking of pledges for political ends. The fact that Western rulers have a comparable doctrine of the reason of state – paternalist utilitarianism – must be concealed as far as possible. A vital part of the factual distortion aspect of deterrence ideology is the ability to pronounce with utter conviction judgments condemning the enemy which in fact apply in every detail also to one's own side.

Examples of this device may be instructive. The reader is advised to substitute the USA for the USSR, and so on, in each passage, a test which is generally useful in this field.

Russia has a long tradition of expansion and the Soviet Union has continued it by extending its influence wherever possible. Of course it can be argued that expansion has been undertaken only in the search for greater security, but one would need enormous confidence in this argument to stake the entire survival of western democracy on it;[19]

She [the USSR] has always followed policies of expedience and I have no doubt that if presented with opportunities where the risks of war were minimal, she would almost certainly take them to extend her political domination as widely as possible.[20]

Reflection on the inversions of these quotations suggests that the only reason the Soviet Union cannot extend her empire as widely as has the USA is that, through various accidents of history, the USA generally happens to have got there first. But in nuclear ideology this must be forgotten, since deterrence does not care to present itself as securing anything as base as the fruits of imperial larceny.

Turning now to inconsistencies and contradictions, the most striking of these is of course well known. Side A's nuclear weapons are to deter Side B from using theirs. But Side B's nuclear weapons will never deter Side A from using theirs, if push comes to shove. (And vice versa.) The implication that nuclear weapons both do and do not deter an enemy from using nuclear weapons is clearly incoherent. Whoever 'we' and 'they' are, if theirs do not deter us, how can we suppose that ours deter them? But if ours do deter them, do not theirs likewise deter us, and may they not suspect as much? Advocates of nuclear deterrence have usually tried to tackle the second horn of the dilemma, known as the self-deterrence problem. A recent Washington treatment of it[21] concluded with utopian hopes for a return to the good old days of a *de facto* American nuclear monopoly, before all the second-best stuff about Mutual Assured Destruction had to be elaborated. This miracle was to be achieved through the early deployment of an effective anti-missile system.[22]

There is a whole group of, at best, inconsistencies which have to do with the mutuality of nuclear threats. Taking them from the point of view of the rulers of Side A, we can see that arming for nuclear deterrence is peaceful and defensive in one's own case, only to become hostile and aggressive as soon as it is the other guy doing it. The balance of terminal threat is said to enhance the probability of peace and stability; but since that same balance requires the permanent possibility of Side A's extinction, perhaps even by accident, it is also undesirable, destabilizing and downright evil. Hence the enormous efforts made by the USA to escape the threat of encroaching mutuality by going for a massive lead in the arms race, known in the jargon of nukespeak by the striking oxymoron of 'a favourable balance'. Taking the wish for the deed, the rulers of Side A like to suppose their own nuclear forces, or even a small part of them such as a particular class of weapon or those of a junior alliance member, can wreak massive devastation on Side B. Side B's weapons are almost, but not quite so effective, thanks to Side A's sensible and effective civil defence preparations. But this in turn dilutes the absolute evil of Side B and its weapons, needed to justify Side A's provisions for exterminating them.

What happens in this shifting and unstable group of contradictions is that a doctrine which professes to desire and embrace a mutuality of nuclear terror, as the only possible basis for security in a Hobbesian international community, keeps breaking out into irrational and partisan asymmetries and immutualities in spite of itself. There may be several causes for this. People let their hopes and loyalties override their theories. They are often unable to stop themselves thinking of a future world war in the misleading way they have been given for understanding the last one. The need to justify arms increases in pseudo-military terms drives them to postulate asymmetries which claim, either that the other side is gaining a significant advantage, or that a new weapon would produce one for their own, or both these things in swift and alternating succession. Then, the rulers of Side A need to prevent their subjects getting too used to nuclear weapons, and are less likely to alert people to their disciplinary functions if they do this by focusing on Side B's weapons rather than on their own. And the rulers of both sides need to avoid reaching any permanent and overt settlement of world domination between them, such as might threaten to undermine the useful institution of having fearful foreign enemies.

But the most probable source of the asymmetry which constantly invades and subverts the professed symmetry and mutuality of nuclear deterrence would be some real asymmetry in the covert but essential functions of nuclear weapons. Such a

157

basis is not far to seek. Given that the rulers of both empires have nuclear weapons and also bunkers, but their subjects for the most part have neither, the apparent contradictions can be read as a veil over something which may be unpleasant but is not contradictory, by the old schoolmen's device of a distinction in terms. Putting matters into crude schematic form, the weapons controlled by the rulers of either side do indeed deter (that is to say terrify) the subjects of both sides, but having no such weapons of their own the subjects are unable to repay the compliment. On the other hand, the weapons of Side A's rulers do not terrorize the *rulers* of Side B as much as they otherwise might, because the latter are provided with bunkers, warning systems, a hot line to their opposite numbers, and of course weapons with which to threaten back until it is too late for threats.[23] The weapons of the rulers of Side B are an embodied act of aggression against the subjects of Side A, and vice versa, as well as serving to cow and divide human beings generally. But for the rulers of Side A their implications are not quite so devastating, and so relations between them and their opposite numbers need never be abandoned. In short, the contradictions and asymmetries which really exist between the two main classes in our global human society are suppressed by treating each mythically separate empire, or sometimes even humankind as a whole, as if it were made up of an undifferentiated mass of equals. And the masked contradictions then re-emerge as doctrinal confusions and inconsistencies in that negation of human universality which is nuclear deterrence.

A looser group of contradictions concerns not the terrorism of nuclear deterrence, but the probability of weapons actually being used in nuclear war.[24] An obvious one with which to begin is the tension between the claim that mutual deterrence makes use of the weapons very unlikely, and the need for each side to convince the other that in certain circumstances it would be absolutely bound to use them. Related to this is a problem about the training of nuclear forces. The weapon whose role is never to be used has to be deployed in the hands of people who are ready to use it at a moment's notice and in ignorance of the reasons for their orders. While these are not strict contradictions, something more like one holds between the view that nuclear weapons make major war highly improbable and the decision that bunkers for military and state personnel are essential. Public opinion polls suggest this confusion is widely shared. The numbers of those who believe a nuclear war is probable within the next twenty years are so great that they must include a large proportion of people who also believe that nuclear deterrence is effective. Within NATO planning and apologetics there are related inconsistencies, such as that nuclear war scenarios can be elaborately forecast and managed, but that uncertainty in nuclear war is a source of security. Or that the enemy is both an unbridled and unintelligent aggressor, and able to make cool and rational calculations of risks and utilities during crisis or war itself. Or that NATO's weapons are only to be used in retaliation, but that NATO retains the right to use them first, that is, to repay something far short of holocaust with Armageddon.

Something more than just the self-deterrence problem under-lies these inconsistencies. And they are not to be resolved as simply as those discussed above. For instance, the rulers of Side A need to convince those of Side B that nuclear war need not happen, that things can be worked out, as for instance in the 1962 Cuba crisis, and that something like the present world system can be maintained indefinitely.[25] (Fond but forlorn hope of rulers in every age.) But they have also to create a flicker of hope to the same effect amongst their own and their enemies' subjects. On the other hand, because the division of the world between rival and hostile empires is a real one, they have also to mean their threats against the enemy, and not merely to parade them for disciplinary effect with their own subjects. A constant, vigorous and wearing equivocation concerning nuclear probabilities has to be propounded by both ruling classes in all directions. One consequence of this may be the very fine adjustment of public shelter and other civil defence programmes in the two super-powers. Enough is done to convince people of the likelihood of nuclear war, but also to sow a few scattered and fitful seeds of selfish hope for survival. But not enough is done to let people think survival is probable, still less take it for granted. Too great a certainty either of survival or of its opposite would corrupt social discipline, the latter through a 'nothing to lose' syndrome.

Other contradictions and inconsistencies in nuclear deterrence must be mentioned more briefly. There is for instance the contradiction of the claim that nuclear disarmament can never be accomplished because the weapons cannot be disinvented with the claim that arms control is possible. For the latter implies that some weapons can be banned by all states, or all mass weapons be denied to some states, or both. The apparent contradiction is resolved by seeing that it involves a tacit distinction between states, with some more equal in respect of the right to prepare genocide than others. Arms control and restraints on proliferation can then be understood as arrangements reached between the two empires for their mutual convenience, as much with respect to their internal affairs as to their global interactions.

Then there is the familiar contradiction of those who urge that disarmament can only be achieved by increase in nuclear weapons, a version of the medieval idea that sin provides God with an occasion for the exercise of grace.[26] Another concerns induction. The absence of major war in Europe since the start of the nuclear age is supposed to prove that the future will continue on the same lines, but the failure of multilateral disarmament negotiations throughout the same period apparently proves nothing of the sort. The claim that nuclear deterrence is an absolute moral evil which must nevertheless be embraced is a graphic example of confusion as to the function of moral reasoning.[27] And the view that both the nuclear arms race and popular opposition to it are causes of dangerous instability in the world system seems uncomfortable to say the least.[28]

Enough has been said to suggest that the last thing we are dealing with, in the doctrines of nuclear deterrence, is straightforward instrumental and prudential reasoning. Yet opposition to nuclear weapons has been very largely based on the mistaken supposition that this was so. It is time to examine the political implications of facing up to that mistake.

V

It has often been remarked that the vice of liberal, reformist political movements, dominated by people from the professional middle classes, is that they raise a clamour against undesirable symptoms or results of the existing social system, but are largely incapable of seeing through to their underlying causes.[29] If they do catch a glimmer of what is really the matter, they are unable to mount effective action to deal with it. They are themselves too deeply imbued with the ideological confusions subserving that against which they protest.

I have already conceded that the aspects of nuclear weapons to which the liberal protest movement objects are both real and really objectionable. But there are drawbacks to mistaking the surface of something, no matter how real a surface it may be, for its inner structure. In the case of the movement for nuclear disarmament this co-option of liberals into the world-view of the pro-nuclear ruling classes, whose clients they are, has far-reaching consequences. Their obsession with nuclear hardware, rather than its origins and functions within the social system, is a classic case of reification which even reinforces the intimidatory role of nuclear weapons. More generally, the traditional case against nuclear deterrence is weakened by the attitude which suggests that humanity's fearful nuclear predicament is the result of something having unaccountably 'gone wrong' in an otherwise rational, progressive and benign social order.[30]

Thus for example it is because they mistake strategic debate about nuclear deterrence for the exercise of honest reason that many disarmers find themselves contributing to a discussion of non-nuclear defence strategies, designed to protect one specious collectivity, 'our side', against that of 'the enemy'. Little seems to be being done to establish some consistency between such activities and the sounder intuition of the peace movement that disarmament requires a principled internationalism from all its advocates.

Or take the assumption that economic activity is mainly about providing use-values for all members of society, but is simply failing to do this in some respects. This is coupled with an old delusion of the Physiocrats, that economic activity is automatically opposed to war and some sort of remedy for it, and ignores the fact that this could only be made true in a society very different from our own. All this underlies the preference, even the irrational requirement, for the conversion of military industries to peaceful purposes to be a politically straightforward affair, no matter what its difficulty or complexity, despite the evidence to the contrary amassed over several decades by Seymour Melman and his associates.[31]

Rip Bulkeley

Another facet of the liberal critique of nuclear deterrence which I suspect takes the pro-nuclear military case far too much at its face value is its interpretation of recent developments, such as the new guidance systems, anti-ballistic missile programmes, and space weapons research, only in terms of a pursuit of first-strike strategic capabilities by both superpowers. Once one realizes that this accusation or aspiration has been around throughout the history of the nuclear debate, one begins to smell a rat so far as its explanatory power with regard to recent events is concerned. It is not that I doubt that first-strikery may be a part, and sometimes an important part, of what is going on. After all, the managers of the arms race are even less likely, on my hypothesis, to see through its surface empirical appearance than are their liberal opponents. But I doubt whether this is a sufficient account of what is producing the world's current drive towards nuclear war. There are grave differences between our present situation and that of twenty years ago, and an explanation which is the same for both just will not do.

What liberals lack, and cannot within their frame of reference discover, is an explanation for why things military 'go wrong' so often and so badly. Whether it be the economic waste or the military lunacy or any other aspect of nuclear deterrence, politicians have to be portrayed as defective in intelligence, imagination, memory and conscience to a degree that is highly implausible. This simplistic story about original sin sets liberals free in their own minds to redeem the world by means of that favourite method of our 'nation of shopkeepers', a little judicious and prudent calculation, appealing to the mythical common sense of one and all. To orient a mass movement around this complaisant fantasy, it is probably important that not too many people should learn much of the history of the nuclear question. For if nuclear deterrence were just a mistake, and pure reason had the powers attributed to it, nuclear weapons should have vanished long ago. The purpose of this article has been to suggest that what nuclear weapons daily achieve for those who command them in the here and now is at least as important for their opponents to understand as what they threaten or destroy. Such understanding involves refusing to take nuclear deterrence on its own misleading, ideological terms.

VI

By way of illustrative postscript, a few remarks applying these ideas to the British Campaign for Nuclear Disarmament may be appropriate. The reluctance of many in CND to oppose nuclear weapons except within the terms of the oppressive social order which requires their existence, so shrewdly remarked by Peggy Duff, can be seen also in recent developments. Acceptance of their rulers' right to defence (that is, to take military action in pursuit of their interests anywhere in the world) has led to the muting or partial abandonment of CND's former opposition to NATO. A new, less radical policy is being promoted which advocates reform of NATO from within, presumably so that it may continue its international dirty work in a slightly more hygienic manner. This fantasy relies essentially on blindness to those aspects of nuclear weapons which go beyond their overt function of strategic deterrence.

Again, whilst there is much verbal radicalism and some militancy of protest in the new wave of CND, its general trend is still towards a lowest common denominator of mere nuclear disarmament, treated as a mysterious recipe for the dissolution of hardware while in most other respects the international political scene is to remain unchanged. It was consistent with this attitude that in 1980 CND in many parts of Britain threw in its lot with the apolitical World Disarmament Campaign, which asked people to put their support behind disarmament negotiations conducted by the rulers of states; that in 1981 it declined to protest publicly against the suppression of Solidarity in Poland; and that in 1982 it could raise no more than a whisper against the harassment of independent Soviet peace campaigners. There is an anguished confusion about a movement which recognizes the revolutionary character of its demands in everything but practice.

Luckily, that is too harsh a judgment. These are only some of the negative sides to a powerful and pluralistic movement. On the positive side should be listed the beginnings of direct action against American nuclear bases, the increasing involvement of conscious working-class organizations, the forging of links between agitation on the nuclear issue and resistance to the economic and social underdevelopment of Britain, and the growth of support for European Nuclear Disarmament, with its

revolutionary and principled opposition to the presence of both
superpowers in Europe. These are some of the seeds of a more
clear-headed nuclear disarmament movement, one which under-
stands how much has to change if nuclear weapons are to be
abolished. If its supporters can realize that the ideological
irrationality of nuclear deterrence is no accident or failure, but
essential to the beast, they will perhaps spend less time trying to
reason things out with their oppressors, and put more effort into
building social forces strong enough to sweep the planet clean of
its nuclear barons[32] and their corrupt intellectual servants.

Notes

1 For accounts of the marxist theory of ideology, see J. Mepham,
'Ideology in *Capital*', *Radical Philosophy*, 1972, no. 2, pp. 12-19; N.
Geras, 'Marx and the Critique of Political Economy', in R.
Blackburn (ed.), *Ideology and Social Science*, London, Fontana,
1972, pp. 284-305; M. Nicolaus, 'The Unknown Marx', in Blackburn,
op. cit., pp. 306-33; F. Jakubowski, *Ideology and Superstructure*,
London, Allison & Busby, 1976; B. Ollman, *Alienation*, Cambridge
University Press, 1976, 2nd edn.
2 This sentence raises a complex of issues in the marxist account of
truth, freedom and social change. I differ from what is widely said to
be the marxist position, by accepting that the knowledge/power/prac-
tice of *all* social classes, and not just that of the exploiters, is subject
to a degree of corruption under capitalism, but that nevertheless
society can be better understood and more effectively transformed
from the vantage point of those who stand to gain least from the
conservation of the existing order.
3 The classic expositions of this theory can be found in K. Marx and F.
Engels, *The German Ideology*, Moscow, Progress, 1968, § 1, and K.
Marx, *Capital*, Moscow, Progress, n.d., Vol. 1. There are of course
differences in ideology between different phases of capitalism, and
between capitalist interpretations of the world and pre-capitalist
ones, which survive most often in the underdeveloped periphery of
international capitalism today.
4 Writers who have made similar points but on their own terms include
G. Anders, N. Chomsky, R. Jungk, M. Kaldor, A. Myrdal and C.
Wright Mills.
5 The resolution of this contradiction via the assumption by the major
multinationals of a practical monopoly over the means of force,
armies, missiles, etc., is fortunately still in its infancy.
6 The designation 'terrorist' is applied after due reflection on the fact
that the weapons in question are supposed to operate by threatening

to take the lives of millions of civilians. The essence of terrorist methods lies, not in the actual killings which they involve for small unofficial forces otherwise lacking in credibility, but in their exercise of terror for political goals against those who are not yet, and may never be, their physical victims.

7 The Soviet-West European gas deal and American grain sales to the USSR are two prominent examples.

8 Deterrence argues that overkill is needed because many warheads might be knocked out by an enemy's first strike. The flaw in this excuse is that modern warning systems enable most if not all of one's missiles to be fired in response after the enemy missiles have been launched but before they arrive. The peace movement's explanation of overkill in terms of a struggle to achieve a first-strike capacity was particularly unconvincing so far as the first boom period for overkill in the 1950s and 1960s was concerned, because of the technical limitations to those weapons and the targeting policies which were adopted accordingly. Neither side's explanation goes any way towards explaining the dogged retention of militarily obsolete nuclear weapons such as (until recently) the V-bombers or Titan, which makes sense, however, when seen in the light of a need to preserve effective high levels of public fear and suspicion.

9 A rough analogy with the marxist idea of relative subsistence levels is intended. However I accept the need to investigate how much internal publicity for nuclear weapons is conducted by the Soviet state, and to ask why China's rulers have not yet gone in for nuclear overkill to any marked degree.

10 Cf. P. Mars, 'La défense civile dans tous ses états', *Interférences*, Paris, 1981, no. 1, pp. 56-62.

11 Transcript of a talk given at Central London Polytechnic, summer 1981.

12 G. Anders, no title, C. Urquhart, (ed.) *A Matter of Life*, London, Cape, 1963, pp. 15-28.

13 The argument behind this claim has to do with their essential need for an underdeveloped periphery in the Third World and for various forms of 'under-class' in the metropolitan heartland, such as women or blacks. Without the massive transfusions of value made possible by these sorts of super-exploitation the system would soon collapse.

14 E.g., from a quick glance in my files, Ian Gilmour, Frank Chapple, Douglas Hurd and William Rodgers.

15 The close parallels between nuclear weapons and god/s, besides having been often invoked by those involved in or narrating their development, will be evident to anyone familiar with L. Feuerbach, *The Essence of Christianity*, New York, Harper & Row, 1957. Appropriate substitutions can be made in countless sentences, as for instance in 'The more empty life is, the fuller, the more concrete is God. The impoverishing of the real world and the enriching of God is one act,' on p. 73.

16 Anders, *op. cit.*, writes as if the capacity for action had really, and not just apparently, shifted from human beings into nuclear weapons. This virtual endorsement of reification reduces his later injunction, that the shift should now be reversed, to idle voluntarism. His mistaken claim that such an apparent shift is not what is meant by reification seems to me to arise from a more fundamental confusion. He treats reification as something that overtakes human beings seen as individuals, whereas the marxist theory is that it happens to human relationships. The distinction is clarified in § 3 of Ollman, *op. cit.*

17 The term is introduced, explained and massively illustrated in G. Lowe, *The Age Of Deterrence*, Boston, Little, Brown, 1964.

18 There is an intended analogy with the marxist idea of a changing ratio between fixed and variable capital, or dead and living labour, in commodity production. A similar thought can be found in M. Kaldor, *The Baroque Arsenal*, London, André Deutsch, 1982. The divergence of time-scales for weapons development and political uses for weapons is particularly striking.

19 Editorial in *The Times*, London, 3 March 1981.

20 Letter in the *Daily Telegraph*, London, 15 February 1982.

21 C. Gray and K. Payne, 'Victory Is Possible', *Foreign Policy*, Washington, 1980, no. 39, cols 14-27.

22 Confirmation that these ideas are gaining official acceptance at the highest level in the USA is given by an article in the *New York Times*, 30 May 1982, pp. 1 and 12.

23 I am attracted by the speculation that this distinction underlies the frequent spectacle of leading statesmen denouncing the nuclear arms race *after* they have lost their privileged position in it. The case of President Eisenhower's parting attack on the 'military-industrial complex', in his farewell speech of January 1961, much quoted by nuclear disarmers, is particularly offensive. For it was the same man who, as US army chief of staff, had set out the doctrine of a partnership between government and business in the military economy back in 1946, a doctrine which was then massively implemented under the Truman administration and his own. His 1946 policy memorandum is published in full in S. Melman, *Pentagon Capitalism*, New York, McGraw Hill, 1970.

24 The link between this second group of ideas, having to do with the objective threat of nuclear weapons, and the first, which has to do with their subjective 'terror', is more a matter for the student of psychology than for an enquiry into ideology as such.

25 Or in other words, nuclear weapons 'cannot be disinvented' because capitalism must not be.

26 E.g. Ministry of Defence, Fact Sheet 3, *Deterrence*, 1981, final sentence: '[Deterrence] . . . gives us time *and incentive* to get international agreement on disarmament measures . . . ' (emphasis added).

27 Most notably and regrettably by M. Walzer in *Just And Unjust Wars*,

102025283032

Harmondsworth, Penguin, 1980. The remark does not of course apply to those who argue that the deterrence function of nuclear weapons makes them morally good.

28 E.g. *The Times, ibid.*
29 E.g. Jakubowski, *op. cit.*, pp. 107-11.
30 'They were basically very British, conservative, and rather naïve. They thought banning the bomb was a fairly simple matter and they never recognized the revolution in British politics that it required. They wanted to get rid of the bomb, leave NATO and abandon the American alliance without upsetting the pattern of life in Sutton, Totnes, or Greenwich, SE3'. P. Duff, *Left, Left, Left*, London, Allison & Busby, 1971, pp. 130-1 and 224-5.
31 Melman, *op. cit.*, and *The Permanent War Economy*, New York, Simon & Schuster, 1974, and many other titles.
32 The phrase is borrowed from P. Pringle and J. Spigelman, *The Nuclear Barons*, London, Michael Joseph, 1982.

Secrecy, Expertise and Democracy

Andrew Belsey

1 Democracy: Theory and Practice

The most widely-known fact of political science is that almost every government in the world claims to be democratic. Democracy is universally acclaimed, even by those régimes which have found it expedient to put it in cold storage. A nice example of this occurred as I was preparing this essay during the early days of the Falkland Islands dispute. Sr Costa Mendez, the Argentinian Foreign Minister, explained to BBC listeners that Argentina had a deep and abiding commitment to democracy, and he indicated that its supension in Argentina was a regrettable though only a temporary episode. And on the other side the British government was constantly stressing that it was going to war only in order to defend democracy, and though this claim needs to be taken with a large dose of South Atlantic salt, clearly the rhetoric of democracy was, as always, powerful. The abuse heaped by the self-confessed champions of democracy on those who dared challenge the wisdom of going to war on this issue made it plain that what is done in The Name of Democracy is Not To Be Questioned. To do justice to the irony of this situation requires a pen more competently satirical than mine.

But what about the reality behind the rhetoric? What about alternative rhetorics? Britain (so runs the official story) is a democracy. That is why we are not only willing to fight countries like Argentina run by 'tinpot fascist juntas' (Mr John Silkin's phrase, I believe) when they invade our space, but are also prepared to defend our democracy against communism, even to the extent of entombing it (and us) in a heap of radioactive rubble. But that is another story. What is democratic about

168

Britain? Politicians are to a fairly limited extent accountable to the people. We still have a system in which a government can be turned out at a general election, although the contest is not usually a fairly balanced one. But it is not being particularly cynical to agree with Rousseau when he pointed out as long ago as 1762 that democracy in Britain means little more than voting every five years. (He actually said 'freedom' rather than 'democracy' because no one could have described Britain's political system in the eighteenth century as democratic.)

To vote occasionally is to accept a minimal amount of participation in the system – it is to accept that your part in the system is only a *minipart*. But isn't democracy supposed to be about participation in a much stronger sense – maximal participation, giving everyone a *maxipart*? But here the inquirer comes up against the alternative rhetorics of democracy. Consider the use of the word 'activist' by the (largely right-wing) press. It is used as a term of disparagement, as if there was something wrong with being a political activist, as if the activist was trying to sneak an unfair political advantage. The use of the word carries the implication that in fact activists are the last people who should be consulted on political matters as they are so far removed from the hearts, minds and lives of ordinary people. The anti-activist rhetoric of the press indicates that ordinary people (the existence of whom is taken for granted) are content in their political apathy and that they are right to be content. And of course professional politicians (who would hate to be confused with activists) are happy to accept this too, as it fits neatly with their own elitist conception of politics.

This sort of simple analysis of popular press rhetoric reveals a definite bias against maxipart democracy, and a position that in its authoritarian leanings might be thought to be in conflict with the dominant ideological insistence on democracy. But what is so tragically fascinating is that this now common disparagement of political involvement and participation is thoroughly in line with the leading academic theory of what democracy actually *is*, a theory which makes both a necessity and a virtue out of *minipart* democracy. Behind the democratic rhetoric is considerable agreement among the popular press shapers of public opinion, practising politicians and academic theorists that democracy just *is* minipart democracy.

Not surprisingly, it is the academic political scientists and political philosophers who have articulated the idea of minipart democracy most thoroughly. Many strands led to the theory, which is not monolithic; nor is it without its critics.[1] The basic idea is simple. People give up any direct participation in politics by voting for parties under the control of strong leaders who make the decisions. Inasmuch as any further participation is allowed by the theory, it is via pressure groups which try to influence political leaders. These intermediate groups are necessary to maintain the pluralist basis of democracy: direct mass participation (it is claimed) would threaten to bring totalitarianism. Competition between parties, however, promotes a stable equilibrium.

In his excellent discussion of various models of liberal democracy, C.B. MacPherson calls this theory of minipart democracy the 'pluralist elitist equilibrium model', each of the descriptive words drawing attention to an important aspect of the theory. It could also be called the economic or even the consumerist theory of democracy since it is based on the market theory of classical economics. Just as manufacturers place their goods before buyers in a competitive market and exchange them for cash, so political parties put their policies before voters in a competitive political 'market' and exchange them for votes. Just as the manufacturer who can respond most effectively to 'what the people want' can make a fortune, so the political party that can respond most effectively to 'what the people want' will obtain political power in virtue of its parliamentary or popular majority.

What is absolutely central to this approach to democracy is that rather than participating in politics directly by being politically active, people become passive consumers of political goods supplied by political parties; their only activity is to vote for the party which promises the greatest return. Integral to this theory of minipart democracy is a theory of human nature: a person as a passive maximizer of satisfactions. And there is also a theory of rationality: to behave rationally is to behave in such a way as to maximize your satisfactions.

Why has this concatenation of ideas that make up the theory of minipart democracy been so popular among theorists? The main justification offered has been that it is *realistic*. This means two things. First that according to political *scientists* it is an accurate description of the way in which the political systems of liberal democracies actually operate; in other words, that the theory is verified in the real world. But of course it is not the job of political *philosophers* simply to accept the way things are now in the real world. They may want to recommend that things should change, and indeed improve. But now the second justification of minipart democracy comes in. Things cannot change all that much because people are not like that. They wish to *maximize* satisfactions but to *minimize* efforts. Minipart democracy makes realistic demands on people; maxipart democracy makes unrealistic demands. People really cannot be bothered with politics; they prefer to leave it to the elites in charge of parties; they are happy so long as they remain fairly inert receivers of (largely material) satisfactions.

Many theorists of democracy are far from content with this minipart account and its various justifications. They see dangers in the elitism and distortions in the view of human beings as passive consumers concerned only with maximizing their satisfactions. The theoretical coherence of the political 'market' can also be questioned. In classical economic theory certain conditions have to be fulfilled before the market can operate properly. Two conditions are especially relevant to the analogy with politics. The first is that potential buyers in the market have to be fully informed – about who is selling, at what price, with what quality. Only then can the buyer make a rational choice. The second condition is that when an offer is made and accepted, there must be an assurance that the contract will be honoured – that the goods ordered, at the right quality, in the correct amount, will actually be delivered. Of course, everyone knows that a model of the market containing both these conditions does not correspond to anything in the real world. Buyers can never be as fully informed as the model demands; for example, there is always a risk the quality will be poorer than in the samples examined (risk is in fact an essential part of classical economic theory). And people are always being cheated out of what they have ordered, especially if they paid in advance.

But if the market model is far too oversimplified to fit the real economic world very well, it fits the real political world even less well. The voter is in a weak position where being cheated is so easy. The voter 'pays in advance'; that is, votes for a party before it delivers the goods. And so often the goods are not delivered – the 'contract' is not fulfilled. The voter votes on the basis of the parties' programmes or manifestoes, but the winning party is under no legal obligation to put the promised policies into operation. The only constraint on the party is that it risks losing the voter's vote next time. But presumably next time it would be rational to vote for a party that at least promised you what you wanted, even if it was unlikely to fulfil the promise, rather than for a party that definitely would not give you what you wanted. And besides, five years in politics is a long time . . . .

The other reason why the 'market' model is inappropriate for politics, and the one that is most important for my purpose here, is that the voter cannot be fully informed and so cannot make a rational choice. Information about policies and proposals is withheld from the general public, and not just accidentally. Official secrecy is a serious and notorious problem in British politics, as is widely recognized.[2] Britain is one of the most secretive – if not *the* most secretive – of the countries that call themselves liberal democracies. And it is not just grave matters of national security that are kept secret. The presumption of both British law and practice is that everything official is secret, however trivial, however important. Publication of official information is a concession, not a duty. Here is a recent example of typical British secrecy: the Secretary of State for Education and Science has refused to tell the House of Commons Select Committee on Education the names of four local authorities which have cut spending on education for the second successive year (and which were criticized anonymously by the Department's inspectors for risking standards). Such information would be of use to MPs, parents, teachers and to voters in the areas concerned. Indeed, without such information it is difficult to see how voters in these areas could cast their votes rationally in the next local authority elections in the manner demanded by the minipart theory of democracy. Voters would simply not have the information necessary to make a rational choice.

The other side of secrecy is the selective release of information, and therefore the manipulation of public opinion. Civil servants would never *lie* (so it is said) but information management is quite another thing! The Falkland Islands dispute provided many examples. First there is news of an incident. Then damage is admitted. Then the possibility of casualties is announced. And finally the details emerge, but with their impact on public opinion defused. The clearest example was probably the news of British casualties suffered when troops going ashore were bombed. The government refused to release details, thus going back on its promise to keep the House of Commons (and therefore the people) informed. (The claim that it was militarily necessary to suppress the information does not seem very plausible.) The details were finally announced, but only in the wake of a victory which would occupy the attention of the media. So bad news is delayed and then announced as a footnote to good news. It is of course only the other side that engages in propaganda: the British government's actions are part of 'defending democracy'. The only conclusion must be that democracy in practice is a long way from the theory.

2 Is an Informed Participatory Democracy Impossible?

It is pretty clear that as far as Britain is concerned even to maintain minipart democracy requires much more openness about information and much less secrecy. And to move on from minipart to maxipart democracy would require a revolution in the treatment and dissemination of information. But it has been claimed that in addition to all the fairly well-known difficulties of maxipart democracy (which boil down to the claim that it is unrealistic) it is actually impossible because paradoxical.

The argument makes use of the concept of an 'informed extreme participatory democracy' (IEPD for short) which is very close to what I mean by a maxipart democracy. An IEPD is 'an organisation in which all (adult) members participate in all the decision making of the organisation' and 'in which all the members have access to all the information relevant to all the decisions that the organisation has to take'.[3] In an IEPD, it is argued, all the state's citizens would know all the state's secrets, including military secrets. And this, it is claimed, is paradoxical.

It is not quite clear exactly what the paradox is. There is no paradox in a secret's being known by a large number of people, as every secret is properly known by someone, and it does not matter how many people properly know a secret; all that matters

173

is that it is not known by those from whom it is being kept. There is no paradox in every citizen of a state knowing that state's military secrets.

But it still might be claimed that a paradox lurks somewhere in this situation. Presumably it is something like this. On the one hand a society desires security and security requires secrecy. But on the other hand, in an IEPD in which everyone had access to all information, military information prejudicial to the society's security would be bound to leak to potential enemies. So the society is committed both to security and to being an IEPD, which prejudices security. So it has contradictory commitments.

But this argument is by no means itself secure. For a start, it depends on two additional assumptions, both of which require much more justification than supposing that they are obvious. The first is that security requires secrecy and the second is that information would be bound to leak to a potential enemy. But even if these assumptions were granted and a contradiction between security and being an IEPD admitted, it does not follow from the mere fact of contradiction that the concept of an IEPD is paradoxical and that it is this concept that must be abandoned. (We may know that two statements are contradictory without knowing which is false.) Politics is a matter of swings and roundabouts. A society might choose to give up some security if it valued being an IEPD very highly. It is also possible that in an IEPD there would be gains in commitment and morale to compensate for some loss of security. This would be a matter of political judgment and choice. It is certainly a long way from being a paradox.

But it should be clear that the way that the 'paradox' was set up had something suspicious about it. It is indeed true that in an IEPD there would be no *state* secrets, because there would be no state. There could be no state. Whatever else it is the state is at least that institution of society which maintains power over society (which it claims is legitimate power, i.e., authority), and in order to do this maintains secrets against the rest of society. With no secrecy there could be no state in this sense. (There could at most be an administration.) But although this is a fairly crude theory of the state it is surely not so crude as, and is in fact a good deal nearer the truth than, Sir Ernest Barker's suggestion that the state 'is not the enemy of Society, but rather stands to it in something of the relation in which a solicitor may stand to a family'.[4] Even today's conservative-liberal minimal-staters do not see the legitimate state in this comfortable way but rather as a disciplinary force, more like a combination of headteacher and (armed) police officer than benign family lawyer.

I am not arguing that maxipart democracy is exactly the same as an IEPD in which *every* citizen participates in *every* decision. Such an 'extreme' democracy would probably not be compatible with likely inclinations, efficiency or enjoyment. What is important in maxipart democracy is that citizens do not just consume the elite's political decisions but are able to participate fully in those decisions which affect or interest them. But there is no paradox in a society organized as a participatory democracy having secrets. It might possibly be inefficient, it might be dangerous, to have secrets so widely disseminated, but it is neither a paradox nor necessarily politically irrational. But the most important point is that there is also no paradox between participatory democracy and the state, because the introduction of participatory democracy challenges the very idea of the state. Obviously as participation increases the state as a secretive and disciplinary institution diminishes.

3 Democracy and the Nuclear State

The increasing of participation and the diminishing of the state is still a distant goal. In the meantime it is important to analyse some of the ways in which state power is maintained. This is especially important in relation to what has become known as the 'nuclear state', because as is becoming increasingly recognized, the nuclear state poses a new and extensive threat to democracy.[5]

In its disciplinary role the state claims a monopoly on two vital means to power, secrecy and expertise. Every bit of information belonging to the state is secret; almost nothing belonging to the individual is. The asymmetry of power can be illustrated by the fact that as more and more personal data go on to computer files, demands for safeguards against misuse through illegitimate access, cross-referencing, collating and analysing fall on deaf ears.[6] The state insists on keeping its secrets, even when they ought to be known to citizens, but demands that individuals hand

Andrew Belsey

over theirs, even when they ought to remain private. The individual is overwhelmed by the power of the state.

It is the same with expertise. Often when a political choice affecting the lives of many people is made there is a pretence that it is a matter only for technical experts: secret state information is processed by state experts who issue some conclusion. This then cannot be (is not allowed to be) challenged, first of all because it is based on secret information and second because it is the conclusion of technical experts and (so it is claimed) therefore above the heads of lay people. This is fundamentally anti-democratic, and there are no democratic procedures available to counteract or contain this reliance on experts, as objectors at planning inquiries into motorways or airport extensions have discovered to their cost.[7]

But reliance on experts for what are in fact matters of political judgment and choice involves a fallacy as old as political philosophy itself, going right back to Plato's analogy between a navigator and a politician. Just as ordinary people leave it to the navigator who has the expertise to steer the ship in the right direction, so they ought to leave the running of society to the politician who has the expertise to direct its course rightly. What is wrong with this is that the navigator does not decide where the ship is steered to; this is decided by someone else (the passengers, say), but given the end the navigator has the means at hand to reach it. So if there is an analogy with politics it is that the politician should have the expertise to administer society along the lines chosen by the people. They choose the end; the politician is concerned solely with means. So Plato's anti-democratic analogy, which depends on confusing technical means with the ends towards which those means are directed, is turned on its head and, properly understood, actually supports democracy.

Of course today it is a bit more complicated. The official story is that the people choose, the experts advise and the politicians decide within the constraints of democracy and expertise. But this is clearly not so on technical matters – and more and more questions of policy are being regarded as technical matters. Neither the people nor their representatives decide where a new motorway or airport is to go – or even whether one is needed. Real decisions are made by experts. It is the same with Concorde or atomic energy.

176

It is also the same with nuclear weapons. In his now (and justly) famous essay Lord Zuckerman blames scientists for the nuclear arms race, though interestingly he removes responsibility from governmental scientific advisers (like himself).[8] Politicians at the top, even aided by the advisers who knew what was going on, have been unable to stem the pressure from below for more and more weapons and newer and more sophisticated systems, pressure aided by economic, political and military interests. For scientists, according to Zuckerman, 'means have a habit of becoming ends'. Or to put it in another way, the technological fix has superseded policy and displaced democratic politics. To blame scientists for the nuclear arms race can hardly be the whole picture, yet it is true that modern expertise lends itself to anti-democratic practices.[9]

The use of secrecy in the nuclear arms race is even more blatantly anti-democratic. As is well known, the original decision to go ahead with a British weapons programme was made in virtual secrecy in 1947 by a small cabinet subcommittee. The only other people who knew about it were the experts. Neither parliament nor the people were consulted or informed. This does not even approach minipart democracy, let alone maxipart democracy. The more recent decision to update Polaris (the Chevaline programme) conforms to the same anti-democratic pattern. When the House of Commons Expenditure Committee got to hear of the decision, again taken in secret by a small cabinet subcommittee, it tried to hold an inquiry into the escalating costs, but the Ministry of Defence, supported by those other ministers who knew the secret, refused to disclose anything. Now Chevaline is likely to be replaced by Trident. This time there has at least been a parliamentary debate. But information about the necessity, purpose and costs of Trident are not available to people so that they can come to their own conclusions. Once again even minipart democracy is a long way off, if not impossible, in the nuclear state.

It is difficult to disagree with one recent writer when he argues for a 'central contention': that 'the existence of nuclear weapons, even without the occurrence of nuclear war, interferes with democratic governance in fundamental ways'.[10] The existence of bipartisan defence policies established within the political elite, the subsequent disallowing of dissent or sceptical voices, secrecy, reliance on expertise, lack of accountability, manipulation of opinion, manufacture of consensus, even deception and coercion – all these have had a dreadful and dulling effect on democratic attitudes and procedures. And for those who still doubt the effects of the nuclear state, Falk quotes this chilling remark, quite open in its anti-democratic insistence:

> In the long run, the existence of nuclear weapons could fundamentally alter government-citizen relations. If, over time, the need of governments to field expansive deterrent forces is not appreciated by citizens who no longer sense a real nuclear threat, popular support for the maintenance of forces could fade – and governments might feel themselves compelled to provide for deterrence without the consent of the governed.[11]

But assuming democracy can survive the Gomperts of this world, and assuming the world can survive, what of the future? The threat of nuclear destruction is the greatest danger the world faces, especially when it is seen, as it must be, as part of an interlocking network of problems, the others being population increase, food shortages, resource depletion and environmental pollution.[12] Although it is action and not just thought that will solve these problems, clear and critical thinking is a necessary precondition of successful action. So another necessary condition is the provision of much more information together with the creating of maxipart democratic structures for discussion and debate. If this is so, then the treatment given to ideas, especially alternative ideas, in Britain at the moment is still a long way from any democratic goal. If one were to take the Falkland Islands dispute as an example, then the future might not seem very hopeful. Quite apart from the rights and wrongs of the matter in morality and international law, not only has it given a major boost to militarism and to imperialism in the good old-fashioned sense of far-flung garrisons with Britannia ruling the waves in between, but it was also the occasion for the abandonment of all critical thinking and for the heaping of abuse on those few sceptics who resisted the tide of 'patriotism'. (Talk of 'one nation' and 'a united people' is inherently anti-democratic. It is also possible to see in it echoes of a particularly obnoxious Nazi war cry.) That the Task Force was launched to save and maintained to boost the Conservative government seems to have become, in spite of its plausibility, literally unspeakable, worse than the foulest obscenity. When serious political ideas get no airing but are greeted by a kind of shocked disbelief and horror quickly followed by abuse, then democracy is in a bad way.

Generalizing on this, what has been witnessed in Britain (and throughout the 'free world') recently has been an extraordinary conspiracy on the part of politicians, press and populace, partly conscious, partly unconscious, to narrow and restrict the boundaries of what are regarded as possible and legitimate ideas and thinking, and hence action, political choices, social arrangements, etc. Not that there has been no opposition. Far from it. But at the same time as an upsurge in radical, oppositional, dissenting or sceptical thought and action, the ideological and repressive fists of the state have tightened even more firmly.

Human energy has not been directed towards solving the world's major problems. Instead, human productive capacities have been fed into the machinery for producing the weapons of (hot) war and its ideological justification, the rhetoric of cold war. This is one reason why organizations like CND, far from deserving vilification as enemies of society, should receive the thanks of genuine democrats everywhere. They are doing the essential work of trying to keep people informed about and aware of the dangers of militarism and nuclear weapons, work that politicians and the press have largely given up on. Even to have minipart democracy much more information needs to be freely available than is provided by the state. By providing information, by raising doubts about official policy, by campaigning to raise consciousness about the dangers of war and the arms race, organizations like CND are performing a great service to democracy.

To make the argument more concrete: for people to come to a rational understanding and assessment of nuclear weapons, without which even minipart democracy is impossible, there would have to be much more information and critical discussion on such topics as:

1 Alternative defence policies and strategies.
2 The arms race, the distribution of weapons and the arms trade.

3 The link between civil and military nuclear power.
4 The problems of nuclear waste transport and disposal.
5 The effects of nuclear war, weapons and fall-out.
6 Likely targets in this country and why they would be targets.
7 Government contingency plans.

The sort of 'information' put forward by the government in *Protect and Survive* was an insult to rational people and a disservice to democracy.

But the sort of informed discussion proposed here would still be possible and necessary even on the assumption that not everything could be open to public scrutiny. Even if one took the view that some secrecy in defence matters was unavoidable, and that some decisions would have to be left in the hands of experts, there would still be a clear difference between military secrets and broad policy issues. To show that some secrecy is necessary is not to justify any amount. So there would still be plenty of scope for genuine public political debate about issues of defence, strategies, and weapons. Above all, in a *democracy* discussion of alternatives to the current orthodoxies should be regarded as essential. And if a commitment to democracy was genuine there would, surely, be a concern to shift issues as far as possible from the secret to the public domain. No such concern is visible in Britain today. In fact, there is just the opposite concern, to strengthen the régime of secrecy and expertise.

The 'official' theory of democracy, minipart democracy, is a pretty poor theory of democracy, yet not even it is anywhere near being realized in the nuclear state, while maxipart democracy, which avoids the dreary idea of people as passive political consumers and gives a value to a people's being politically involved and active, seems a long way away. The anti-democratic, authoritarian tendencies of the modern state have been well assessed by Margolis:

> The official doctrines of fascism were discredited following the holocaust of the Second World War, but the notion that the citizen's patriotic duty requires acquiescence to the superior wisdom of his political leaders has come to be used regularly to attack [him], whenever he criticises his government's current policies.[13]

The dangers of fascism are even greater in the nuclear state. Modern politics, through its use of secrecy, expertise and other weapons in the ideological war, has diminished democracy and brought the world to the edge of oblivion. Perhaps it is time to try an alternative – time to trust the people.

Notes

1 C.B. Macpherson, *The Life and Times of Liberal Democracy* (Oxford University Press, 1977), ch. 4; Michael Margolis, *Viable Democracy* (Penguin, 1979).
2 David Leigh, *The Frontiers of Secrecy* (Junction Books, 1980); James Michael, *The Politics of Secrecy* (Penguin, 1982); Patricia Hewitt, *The Abuse of Power: Civil Liberties in the United Kingdom* (Martin Robertson, 1982), ch. 4.
3 W.A. McMullen, 'Censorship and Participatory Democracy: A Paradox', *Analysis*, 32 (1972), pp. 207-8. For a response see H.M. Jones, 'Censorship, State Secrets and Participatory Democracy', *Analysis*, 33 (1973), pp. 143-44.
4 Ernest Barker, *Principles of Social and Political Theory* (Oxford University Press, 1951), p. 276.
5 Robert Jungk, *The Nuclear State* (Calder, 1979); Martin H. Ryle, *The Politics of Nuclear Disarmament* (Pluto Press, 1981), ch. 4; Gari Donn (ed.), *Missiles, Reactors and Civil Liberties* (Scottish Council for Civil Liberties, 1981); Richard Falk, 'Nuclear Weapons and the End of Democracy', *Praxis International*, 2 (1982), pp. 1-11; and many of the writings of E.P. Thompson.
6 Andrew Belsey, 'The Delicate Balance of Progress and Privacy', *Computing*, 7 (47) (1979), pp. 444-5; Hewitt, *op. cit.*, pp. 34-41. The recent White Paper, *Data Protection* (Cmnd 8539, HMSO, 1982), is not an adequate response to the problem.
7 J.R. Lucas, *Democracy and Participation* (Penguin, 1976).
8 Lord Zuckerman, *Science Advisers, Scientific Advisers and Nuclear Weapons* (Menard Press, 1980).
9 An excellent and stimulating discussion of this can be found in Nicholas Maxwell, *What's Wrong With Science?* (Bran's Head Books, 1976). See esp. pp. 6, 157 and 192.
10 Falk, *op. cit.*, p. 2.
11 David C. Gompert *et al.*, *Nuclear Weapons and World Politics* (McGraw-Hill, 1977), quoted by Falk, *op. cit.*, p. 2.
12 For an interesting though pessimistic and anti-democratic account of these interlocking problems see Robert Heilbroner, *An Inquiry into the Human Prospect* (Calder & Boyars, 1975).
13 Margolis, *op. cit.*, p. 11.

Index

absence of war between great
powers, 43
activist, 169
anarchism, 101
Anders, G., 151, 153, 164
anti-activist press, 169
anti-Marxist strategy, 10
area bombing, switch to, 17
Argentina, 168
Aristotle, 131
arms race, 152
Athens, moral principle, 27
Auden, W.H. (quoted), 141

baby-on-car-bumper argument,
105, 106, 120, 122-9 *passim*
balancing risks and costs, 5
Barker, E., 174
Barnaby, F., 63
Bell, Bishop G.K.A., 37, 40
Belsey, A., 181
Berlin crisis (1959), 96
'better red than dead', 12-27
biological survival, 7
blackmail, nuclear, 25-6
bluff: policy, 5, 22-3, 23-4; nuclear
deterrence not based on, 43-4
Bolsover, P., 98
Britain: base for country possessing nuclear weapons, 38;
changes in practice of war, 30-1;
complicity in US use of nuclear
weapons, 36; control centres, 87;

Home Office booklet *Protect and
Survive* (1980), 7, 19, 87, 90;
Home Office circulars, 88, 98;
Home Office data, 87; Home
Office self-deception, 92;
independent nuclear deterrent,
43; local government officers as
survivors, 133-4; Ministry of
Defence, 89; one-off attack, 90;
possession of nuclear weapons,
38; rehearsals for doomsday, 87;
warning of nuclear attack, 89;
wartime administration, 87, 133-4
Brown, H., 56, 66
Bukharin, N.I., 147

Campaign for Nuclear Disarmament (CND), 117, 163, 179; 'ban
the bomb' slogan, 108; core of
shared ideas, 119
Carter, J., 46, 56
casuistry, 34-5
casuists, 8-9, 119-29 *passim*; pro-
nuclear, 123
central contention, 177
Chalfont, Lord, 22
Chevaline warhead, 51, 177
Chile, post-Allende, 39
chivalrous ideal, 29-30
Chomsky, N., 151, 164
Christian attitude to war, 30
circular error probable (CEP), 64
cities: as centres of state power,

51; devastation of, 16, 36; innocent inhabitants, 54
civil defence, 86-92
civilian populations, massacre of, 16, 36
civil society, 93
CND, *see* Campaign for Nuclear Disarmament
collateral deterrence, 6, 59
collective death, 141
Collins, H.M., 85
colonial subjects, treatment of, 34
committed moral argument, 118
communist domination, 24; life risked to prevent, 14
Communist Party, 13
Congress of International Physicians for the Prevention of Nuclear War, 97-8
conscripts, status of, 55-6
Copi, I.M., 78-80
counter-force strategy, 17, 51, 56, 57
counter-silo strikes, 51-2
countervalue strategy, 17, 51
credibility of deterrence policy, 106
credibility of participants, 4
cruise missiles, 3, 89, 112
crusaders, 8-9, 119-29 *passim*
crusading religious war doctrine, 60
Cuba crisis (1962), 159
Czechoslovakia, defiance in, 74

Dando, M., 98
Data Protection (1982), 181
Dean, H., 84
death preferred to communism, 12, 13-14
defence deterrence, 50
defence policies, irrationality of, 109
defenders of deterrent, 24
democracy: informed participatory, 173-5; maxipart, 11, 169, 171; minipart, 11, 169, 170-1; nuclear state and, 175-81; theory/practice, 168-73
democratic institutions, reform of, 10-11
deterrence ideology, 10, 115
Dolan, P.J., 98
Donn, G., 181
drawing the line, 34-5
Dresden, bombing of, 104
Duff, P., 163

economic theory, classical, 171
Eisenhower, D.D., 166
Electro-Magnetic Pulse (EMP), 90
El Salvador, 39
emotionalism, charge of, 9, 120-1, 122
enemy: attitudes to, 27; insane, 25; nuclear attack on population, 19
Europe: nuclear war limited to, 116; Soviet occupation of, 38-9
European Nuclear Disarmament, 163-4
existence, complexity and richness, 94-5
experts, 11, 176; advisers to policy makers, 82-3; accreditation, 7; cognitive authority, 78-84; failure to agree, 80, 83

Falk, R., 66, 178
Falkland Islands dispute, 172-3, 178-9
financial cost of weapons system, 24
firebreak, 47
first-strike attack, 5, 20, 21
flexible response strategy, 42, 115, 116
Ford, J.C., 54, 65
Foucault, M. (quoted), 67
France, 76, 81-2
Freedman, L., 63
freedom fighter, 32

Geneva Conventions (1949), 60, 66, 102
Geneva Protocols (1977), 61, 63-4

Germany: bombing raids by, 31; rehabilitation, 21
Gilpin, R., 82
Glasstone, S., 98
Gleisner, J., 98
Gompert, D.C., 181
Goodwin, G., 63
Goodwin, P., 98
Greece, colonels' regime, 39
Grotius, H., 55
Guatemala, 39
guerilla, 32
guilt, imputation of, 53

Harvey, B., 85
Hatfield, M.O., 27
Hegel, G.W.F., 145
Heilbroner, R., 181
Hewitt, P., 181
high-power emission, 90
Hiroshima, 17, 36-7, 67
Hobbes, T., 93, 98, 157
Hockaday, A., 63
hostage deterrence, 50-1
human civilization, jeopardization of, 94-7, 139
human life, dimensions of, 94-5
Hungary, defiance in, 74

ideology, 145
Ik, the, 130, 132, 137, 141
imperialisms, 147-8
India, 47
informed extreme participatory democracy (IEPD), 173-5
innocence, 54
innocent, killing of, 16
international crisis, emotional reactions in, 48
International Institute of Strategic Studies, 71
international laws of war, 6, 41, 56
international nuclear disarmament, 68
international nuclear-free zone, 68
intuition(s), 129; conflicting, 35
inversion, 10, 150-1

Iraq, 47
Israel, 47

Japan: nuclear bombing, 17, 36-7, 67; rehabilitation, 21
Jerusalem, massacre of inhabitants, 30
Job, 134
Johnson, J.T., 65, 66
Jones, H.M., 181
Jungk, R., 181
just war doctrine, 5, 6, 14-18 *passim*, 59-61; philosophers on, 15; principles of international morality, 41; reasonable terms to enemy, 33; theologians on, 15

Kafka, F. (quoted), 144
Kahn, H., 99
Kaldor, M., 84
Kennedy, E., 20
Khrushchev, N.S., 67
Kissinger, H., 39
Kistiakowsky, G., 63
Korean war, 33

La Roque, G.R., 63
launch-on-warning plans, 45, 46
law of excluded middle, 34, 35
legitimate acts of war, 35
Leigh, D., 181
Lenin, V.I., 147
lesser of two evils argument, 49
liberal protest movement, 161-2
Libya, 47
Liebnecht, W., 147
life, meaning given to, 134
life-maintaining services, disruption of, 88
Locke, J., 93, 98
Lucas, J.R., 181

McCabe, H., 23
McMullen, W.A., 181
McNamara, R., 17, 56
MacPherson, C.B., 170
Margolis, M., 180, 181

Mars, P., 165
Marx, K. and marxism, 145; class war concept, 10; critiques of capitalism, 147; resources, 10; theory of ideology, 164
mass murder, 36
Maxwell, N., 181
Mazur, A., 85
Measor, N., 111
Melman, S., 161
Mendez, C., 168
Michael, J., 181
Middle Ages, warfare and chivalry, 16, 55-6
military chain of command, 23
military profession, 23
MIRVd missiles, 45
Montana, silos in, 18
moral counter-force deterrence theory, 59
morality, 9, 134-5; applied to governments, 36; of nuclear deterrence, 2; and survival, choice between, 137-8; of threats, 49-50
morals, 16
Mountbatten, Lord, 63
murder, 33
MX missile, 3, 112

Nagasaki, 17, 36-7, 67
NATO: anti-tank weapons, 75, 76; Greek exercise, 39; intermediate range missiles, 153; nuclear policy, 49, 70, 159; nuclear weapons deployed to counter those of USSR, 154; offensive capability, 75; option first use, 44; Tornado programme, 155
natural state, 93
Neild, R., 77
Nelkin, D., 85
neutron warhead, 84
non-combatants, 31; deliberate killing, 16, 53; distinction from combatants, 16-17; immunity of, 6
Non-proliferation Treaty, 47

non-resistance to aggression, 42
nuclear attack, circumstances warranting, 105
nuclear deterrence: arguments supporting, 41-8; as degenerative state, 46-7; ideology, 10, 115, 146; inconsistencies, contradictions, 156-60 *passim*; legitimate, 57-8; stability of system, 44-8
nuclear state, economic/social relations, 10
nuclear strategy, thinking rationally about, 110
nuclear war, limited, 6, 104, 115
nuclear weapons: accidental use, 45; cost, 111, 150; functional changes in society, 150; god/s and, 165; as guarantee of world peace, 152; illusion of independence, 111; limited explosive power/low radiation effects, 103; moral wickedness of possession, 6; proliferation to other countries, 47; protection by someone else's, 112-13; small scale use, 115, 117; stockpiling, 18, 20; tactical battlefield, 47, 52

overkill, 165
Owen, D., 51

pacifists, 14, 101
Pakistan, 47
Pascal, B., 136
Paskins, B., 62
Peace of God, 55
Pershing II missiles, 3, 45, 112
physiocrats, 161
Plato, 176
pluralist elitist equilibrium model, 170
Poland, 17, 74, 149, 163
Polaris missiles, 51, 86, 177
police forces, 16
politicians: accountability, 169; lying by, 37
Pol Pot, 39

Pope Pius XII, 32
Poseidon fleet, 155
preservation of species, 131-2
Prisoners' Dilemma, 111, 112
prisoners of war, 31
private shelter business, 98
property, as theft, 119, 121, 122
proportionality, 56-8
Protect and Survive (1980), 7, 87, 90
Pugwash Conference on Science and World Affairs (1981), 97

radiation effects, 52, 88, 103; delayed fallout, 89; scale, danger of fallout, 7
Ramsey, P., 57, 65, 66, 105
rationality, breakdown of, 58, 62
Ravetz, J., 85
Reagan, R., 3
reification, 10, 145, 152, 153, 166
retaliatory strike, 5, 20-1
Rogers, P., 98
Romania, status of, 26
Rousseau, J.J., 169
rules of war, 15-16; in Second World War, 31
Russell, B., 25
Ryle, Sir M., 63
Ryle, M.H., 181

Salmon, W.C., 78-80, 85
Schell, J., 98
Schwarzenberger, G., 53
second-strike attack, 20, 21
Second World War, 6; as just war, 17, 103; bombing of German cities, 104; switch to area bombing, 17
secrecy, governmental, 11, 109-10, 172
self-defence, killings in, 33
Sève, L., 98
Sherman, General W.T., 102
sick, help for, in nuclear aftermath, 142
significant choice, 140-1

social reality, unity with ideological appearances, 146
society, post-holocaust, 7, 88-9, 92-3, 96
soldier, responsibility of, 38
South Africa, 47; black people in, 39
Soviet Union (USSR): before/after nuclear attack, 21; belief that US aims at world domination, 26; Czechoslovakia, occupation of, 38; domination over rest of Europe, 38; garrison troops in 'colonies', 76; gas deal with West Europe, 165; global domination aim, 68-9; harassment of peace campaigners, 163; Hungary, occupation of, 38; as military threat, 1; morale in army, 74, 76-7; political system, 77; superiority in men and weapons, 70; technological inferiority, 77; threat to Europe, 75-7, 81-2
SS20s, 3
state: employment by, 148; information of citizens, 11; surveillance, intimidation, indoctrination by, 148
Statement on Defence Estimates (UK 1980), 69
Suarez, F., 55
surgical strike, 50
survival: language of, 92; necessities of, 137; point of, 134
survivors, numbers of, 88
'Suvurov, V.', 74

target, soft/hard, 17
targeting war recovery capability, 90
Taylor, A.J.P., 63
terminal deterrence, 153
terrorism, 32; nuclear deterrence as, 6
terrorist, 32, 164-5; captured, attitude of, 36

Thatcher, M., 2, 3, 33
thrift, 131
Titan, 165
Travis, G.D.L., 85
Trident, 3, 177
Truman, H.S., 36
Tucker, A., 98
Turnbull, C., 129-30

unconditional surrender of enemy,
  15; of Germany, 33
under-class, 165
unilateral disarmament, 8, 24;
  arguments against, 25; by
  Western powers, 26
unilateralist, 22
United States: before/after nuclear
  attack, 21; belief that USSR aims
  at world domination, 26;
  Congress report (1981), 62-3;
  destabilizing/wrecking neutralist
  economies, 38; grain sales to
  USSR, 165; menace to freedom
  of other countries, 39; only
  nation to have used nuclear
  weapons, 36; strategic defence, 3
units of capital, globally
  agglomerated, 149
Urals, silos in, 18
USSR, *see* Soviet Union

Van den Dungen, F., 98
Vattel, E. de, 55
V-bombers, 165
victory, war not justified by, 15
Vitoria, F. de, 55

Walzer, M., 102, 105-6, 166-7

war: continued occurrence, 29;
  impersonal event, 14-15; instrument of policy, 15; making
  impossible, 40; moral justification, 15; not justified by victory,
  15; part of human existence, 28;
  self-generating event, 25; total,
  17, 31, 53-4
war crime, definition of, 104
war crimes trials, 32, 104
warning shot, 50
Warsaw: as Ground Zero, 27;
  sufferings of inhabitants, 27
Warsaw Pact countries: lack of
  freedom, 19; puppets of USSR,
  26; standard of living, 19; tank
  numbers/efficiency, 71-4; *see also*
  Soviet Union
Western Nations: freedoms, 19;
  standard of living, 19
West Germany, limited nuclear
  war study, 52
wickedness, monstrous acts of
  drive perpetrator insane, 36
wives, as slaves, 119, 121-2
workers: mistrust in rival empires,
  150; treatment of, 148
World Disarmament Campaign,
  163
world government, believers in,
  28-9
wrong, worse to do than suffer, 5,
  27
wrong to threaten what is wrong to
  do, 37

Zuckerman, Lord, 51, 63, 64, 112,
  177